Citroën
DS

Malcolm Bobbitt

VELOCE PUBLISHING
THE PUBLISHER OF FINE AUTOMOTIVE BOOKS

Also from Veloce Publishing

SpeedPro Series

4-Cylinder Engine - How to Blueprint & Build a Short Block for High Performance by Des Hammill
Alfa Romeo Twin Cam Engines - How to Power Tune by Jim Kartalamakis
BMC 998cc A-Series Engine - How to Power Tune by Des Hammill
BMC/Rover 1275cc A-Series Engines - How to Power Tune by Des Hammill
Camshafts - How to Choose & Time them for Maximum Power by Des Hammill
Cylinder Heads - How to Build, Modify & Power Tune Updated & Revised Edition by Peter Burgess
Distributor-type Ignition Systems - How to Build & Power Tune by Des Hammill
Fast Road Car - How to Plan and Build New Edition by Daniel Stapleton
Ford SOHC 'Pinto' & Sierra Cosworth DOHC Engines - How to Power Tune Updated & Enlarged Edition by Des Hammill
Ford V8 - How to Power Tune Small Block Engines by Des Hammill
Harley-Davidson Evolution Engines - How to Build & Power Tune by Des Hammill
Holley Carburetors - How to Build & Power Tune New Edition by Des Hammill
Jaguar XK Engines - How to Power Tune New Edition by Des Hammill
MG Midget & Austin-Healey Sprite - How to Power Tune Updated Edition by Daniel Stapleton
MGB 4-Cylinder Engine - How to Power Tune by Peter Burgess
MGB - How to Give your MGB V8 Power Updated & Revised Edition by Roger Williams
MGB, MGC & MGB V8 - How to Improve by Roger Williams
Mini Engines - How to Power Tune on a Small Budget 2nd Edition by Des Hammill
Motorsport - Getting Started in by SS Collins
Nitrous Oxide by Tervor Langield
Rover V8 Engines - How to Power Tune by Des Hammill
Sportscar/Kitcar Suspension & Brakes - How to Build & Modify Enlarged & Updated 2nd Edition by Des Hammill
SU Carburettors - How to Build & Modify for High Performance by Des Hammill
Suzuki 4WD by John Richardson
Tiger Avon Sportscar - How to Build Your Own Updated & Revised 2nd Edition by Jim Dudley
TR2, 3 & TR4 - How to Improve by Roger Williams
TR5, 250 & TR6 - How to Improve by Roger Williams
V8 Engine - How to Build a Short Block for High Performance by Des Hammill
Volkswagen Beetle Suspension, Brakes & Chassis - How to Modify for High Performance by James Hale
Volkswagen Bus Suspension, Brakes & Chassis - How to Modify for High Performance by James Hale
Weber DCOE, & Dellorto DHLA Carburetors - How to Build & Power Tune 3rd Edition by Des Hammill

Those were the days ... Series

Alpine Rallies by Martin Pfunder
Austerity Motoring by Malcolm Bobbitt
Brighton National Speed Trials by Tony Gardiner
British Police Cars by Nick Walker
Crystal Palace by Sam Collins
Dune Buggy Phenomenon by James Hale
Dune Buggy Phenomenon Volume 2 by James Hale
Motor Racing at Brands Hatch in the Seventies by Chas Parker
Motor Racing at Goodwood in the Sixties by Tony Gardiner
Promotional Vehicles by James Hale
Three Wheelers by Malcolm Bobbitt

Enthusiast's Restoration Manual Series

Citroën 2CV, How to Restore by Lindsay Porter
Classic Car Body Work, How to Restore by Martin Thaddeus
Classic Cars, How to Paint by Martin Thaddeus
Triumph TR2/3/3A, How to Restore by Roger Williams
Triumph TR4/4A, How to Restore by Roger Williams
Triumph TR5/250 & 6, How to Restore by Roger Williams
Triumph TR7/8, How to Restore by Roger Williams
Volkswagen Beetle, How to Restore by Jim Tyler

Essential Buyer's Guide Series

Alfa GT Buyer's Guide by Keith Booker
Alfa Romeo Spider by Keith Booker
E-Type Buyer's Guide
Porsche 928 Buyer's Guide by David Hemmings
VW Beetle Buyer's Guide by Richard Copping

Auto Graphics Series

Fiat & Abarth by Andrea & David Sparrow
Jaguar MkII by Andrea & David Sparrow
Lambretta Ll by Andrea & David Sparrow

General

AC Two-litre Saloons & Buckland Sportscars by Leo Archibald
Alfa Romeo Berlinas (Saloons/Sedans) by John Tipler
Alfa Romeo Giulia Coupè GT & GTA by John Tipler
Alfa Tipo 33 by Ed McDonough
Anatomy of the Works Minis by Brian Moylan
Armstrong-Siddeley by Bill Smith
Autodrome by Sam Collins
Automotive A-Z, Lane's Dictionary of Automotive Terms by Keith Lane
Automotive Mascots by David Kay & Lynda Springate
Bentley Continental, Corniche and Azure by Martin Bennett
BMW 5-Series by Marc Cranswick
BMW Z-Cars by James Taylor
British 250cc Racing Motorcycles by Chris Pereira

British Cars, The Complete Catalogue of, 1895-1975 by Culshaw & Horrobin
Bugatti Type 40 by Barrie Price
Bugatti 46/50 Updated Edition by Barrie Price
Bugatti 57 2nd Edition by Barrie Price
Caravans, The Illustrated History 1919-1959 by Andrew Jenkinson
Caravans, The Illustrated History from 1960 by Andrew Jenkinson
Chrysler 300 - America's Most Powerful Car 2nd Edition by Robert Ackerson
Citroën DS by Malcolm Bobbitt
Cobra - The Real Thing! by Trevor Legate
Cortina - Ford's Bestseller by Graham Robson
Coventry Climax Racing Engines by Des Hammill
Daimler SP250 'Dart' by Brian Long
Datsun 240, 260 & 280Z by Brian Long
Dune Buggy Files by James Hale
Dune Buggy Handbook by James Hale
Fiat & Abarth 124 Spider & Coupé by John Tipler
Fiat & Abarth 500 & 600 2nd edition by Malcolm Bobbitt
Ford F100/F150 Pick-up 1948-1996 by Robert Ackerson
Ford F150 1997-2005 by Robert Ackerson
Ford GT40 by Trevor Legate
Ford Model Y by Sam Roberts
Funky Mopeds by Richard Skelton
Honda NSX by Brian Long
Jaguar, The Rise of by Barrie Price
Jaguar XJ-S by Brian Long
Jeep CJ by Robert Ackerson
Jeep Wrangler by Robert Ackerson
Karmann-Ghia Coupè & Convertible by Malcolm Bobbitt
Land Rover, The Half-Ton Military by Mark Cook
Lea-Francis Story, The by Barrie Price
Lexus Story, The by Brian Long
Lola - The Illustrated History (1957-1977) by John Starkey
Lola - All The Sports Racing & Single-Seater Racing Cars 1978-1997 by John Starkey
Lola T70 - The Racing History & Individual Chassis Record 3rd Edition by John Starkey
Lotus 49 by Michael Oliver
Mazda MX-5/Miata 1.6 Enthusiast's Workshop Manual by Rod Grainger & Pete Shoemark
Mazda MX-5/Miata 1.8 Enthusiast's Workshop Manual by Rod Grainger & Pete Shoemark
Mazda MX-5 (& Eunos Roadster) - The World's Favourite Sportscar by Brian Long
Mazda MX-5 Miata Roadster by Brian Long
MGA by John Price Williams
MGB & MGB GT - Expert Guide (Auto-Doc Series) by Roger Williams
Micro Caravans by Andrew Jenkinson
Mini Cooper - The Real Thing! by John Tipler
Mitsubishi Lancer Evo by Brian Long
Morgan Drivers Who's Who - 2nd International Edition by Dani Carew
Motor Racing Reflections by Anthony Carter
Motorhomes, The Illustrated History by Andrew Jenkinson
Motorsport in colour, 1950s by Martyn Wainwright
MR2 - Toyota's Mid-engined Sports Car by Brian Long
Nissan 300ZX & 350Z - The Z-Car Story by Brian Long
Pass the Driving Test by Clive Gibson & Gavin Hoole
Pontiac Firebird by Marc Cranswick
Porsche Boxster by Brian Long
Porsche 356 by Brian Long
Porsche 911 Carrera by Tony Corlett
Porsche 911R, RS & RSR, 4th Edition by John Starkey
Porsche 911 - The Definitive History 1963-1971 by Brian Long
Porsche 911 - The Definitive History 1971-1977 by Brian Long
Porsche 911 - The Definitive History 1977-1987 by Brian Long
Porsche 911 - The Definitive History 1987-1997 by Brian Long
Porsche 911 - The Definitive History 1997 on by Brian Long
Porsche 911SC Companion by Adrian Streather
Porsche 914 & 914-6 by Brian Long
Porsche 924 by Brian Long
Porsche 933 Companion by Adrian Streather
Porsche 944 by Brian Long
RAC Rally, Illustrated History of by Tony Gardiner
Rolls-Royce Silver Shadow/Bentley T Series Corniche & Camargue Revised & Enlarged Edition by Malcolm Bobbitt
Rolls-Royce Silver Spirit, Silver Spur & Bentley Mulsanne 2nd Edition by Malcolm Bobbitt
Rolls-Royce Silver Wraith, Dawn & Cloud/Bentley MkVI, R & S Series by Martyn Nutland
RX-7 - Mazda's Rotary Engine Sportscar (updated & revised new edition) by Brian Long
Secret Abingdon by Stuart Turner, Marcus Chambers, Peter Browning & Philip Young
Singer Story: Cars, Commercial Vehicles, Bicycles & Motorcycles by Kevin Atkinson
Subaru Impreza by Brian Long
Taxi! The Story of the 'London' Taxicab by Malcolm Bobbitt
Triumph Motorcycles & the Meriden Factory by Hughie Hancox
Triumph Speed Twin & Thunderbird Bible by Harry Woolridge
Triumph Tiger Cub Bible by Mike Estall
Triumph Trophy Bible by Harry Woolridge
Triumph TR6 by William Kimberley
Turner's Triumphs, Edward Turner & his Triumph Motorcycles by Jeff Clew
Velocette Motorcycles - MSS to Thruxton Updated & Revised Edition by Rod Burris
Volkswagen Bus or Van to Camper, How to Convert by Lindsay Porter
Volkswagens of the World by Simon Glen
VW Beetle Cabriolet by Malcolm Bobbitt
VW Beetle - The Car of the 20th Century by Richard Copping
VW Bus, Camper, Van, Pickup by Malcolm Bobbitt
VW - The air-cooled era by Richard Copping
Works Rally Mechanic by Brian Moylan

First published in 2005 by Veloce Publishing Limited, 33 Trinity Street, Dorchester DT1 1TT, England. Fax 01305 268864/e-mail info@veloce.co.uk/web www.veloce.co.uk or www.velocebooks.com
ISBN 1-904788-30-0/UPC 36847-00330-2
British Library Cataloguing in Publication Data - A catalogue record for this book is available from the British Library. Typesetting, design and page make-up all by Veloce Publishing Ltd on Apple Mac. Printed in Italy.

Visit Veloce on the web - www.veloce.co.uk

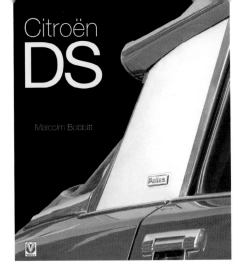

Citroën DS

Malcolm Bobbitt

CONTENTS

FOREWORD

**By Graham Hull M. Des, RCA
Chief Stylist Rolls-Royce Motor
Cars and Bentley Motor Cars
1984-2001**

THE AESTHETIC PERSPECTIVE

Analysing the Citroën DS from a styling or design viewpoint is slightly intimidating; after all, it's unusual for a motor car to be referred to as a Goddess, and a reputed 12,000 orders on the first day of its launch must be unprecedented. Renowned philosopher, Roland Barthes, was inspired by the new Citroën to write a eulogy, famously comparing the car with modern-day cathedrals. In 1999 a UK design jury declared the DS 'The Product of the Century', ahead of other well-known consumables.

It is hard to think of many other vehicles which have equalled the Citroën's initial impact and impact on public awareness. Intriguingly, in the car world, this Goddess is not always assured of unreserved adoration. A 1997 survey of the top twenty most beautiful cars, conducted by *Classic and Sportscar* magazine, placed the DS at number eighteen; I suspect that it is among the wider design world and art connoisseurs that this vehicle finds its most ardent admirers.

STYLING BACKGROUND

The conceptual origins of a car launched in 1955 would have been around five years earlier; in Citroën's case, full size mock-ups bearing DS DNA were being worked on in 1948. Citroën's Italian chief stylist, Flaminio Bertoni, had been involved with the 1934 *Traction Avant* and later the 2CV. Bertoni, a true backroom boy, was a talented artist in not only two dimensions but three: it was his sculptural skills that held the key to the DS's radical visual solution to a number of design issues.

Motor car styling was breaking with tradition in the 1930s. Streamlining began to have a stylistic influence on everything from trains, through domestic appliances, to cars. French car designers appeared to welcome the *avant-garde* influence of aerodynamics. For instance, in 1938 the Parisian coachbuilder, Pourtout, created the superb low-drag Georges Paulin-styled Embiricos Bentley that raced at Le Mans. World War Two prevented much progress although aircraft aerodynamics surged ahead. In the 1950s Panhard cars became aerodynamic, also competing at Le Mans. No-one, however, seems to have been more committed to this new discipline than Citroën.

From the earliest post war sketches and models it is obvious that Bertoni had decided that a windcheating philosophy was to be the *raison d'etre* for his new big Citroën. What is also apparent is that, unusually, Citroën's engineering designers must have totally agreed with the stylist's quest. Major changes were made to accommodate aesthetic requirements, an example being that the wheelbase was increased until it reached a staggering 10ft 3in, exactly the same as that of a Rolls-Royce Silver Cloud! The DS's rear track was also modified until it was 8in narrower than the front.

The main styling elements were in place by December 1950, when Project D was officially born. It must be reassuring to today's designers that Bertoni was still deciding exterior and interior elements six months before the

'Spaceship styling' is often the term used to describe the DS. The family depicted in this almost bizarre publicity item might well look at the exhibit in wonder when it was displayed in Milan in October 1957. (Author's collection)

car's launch. It's worth remembering that designs before 1950, and to some extent to this day, relied primarily on conception by drawn elevation. That's to say, a side view was drawn first, followed by front and back views. It was then usually necessary to experiment with how best to join the corners. Increasing reliance on clay models, and nowadays computers, too, have helped to develop car shapes 'in the round'. Bertoni's sculptural skills definitely put him ahead of the game. Legend has it that he fashioned the basic form of the *Traction Avant* in plasticine during one session.

STYLING - EXTERIOR AESTHETICS

It's a cliché to claim that something is ahead of its time - and also a contradiction, although the DS may be the exception that proves the rule. Like all good ideas the DS's style is based on a simple premise or theme, and in this case it was the knowledge that nature's most aerodynamic shape is the teardrop. The end result was essentially a streamlined egg shape with a flattened base, the main intrusions being the windscreen, headlamps, and wheel openings.

One can only admire Bertoni's ruthless, focused pursuit of this ideal. Previously, some designers had attempted to generally round car bodies to a greater or lesser degree. The Citroën did it so wholeheartedly that the final form is still pretty well unique. The dramatic side profile is unforgettable and, significantly, the visual impact of the wheels is almost irrelevant to the DS's presence, something few modern cars can claim.

Since 1955 some of the DS's visual aspects have become so much a part of mainstream design that it's difficult now to appreciate just how revolutionary these were. From the low, rounded nose of the integrated bumper and minimal air intake, the broad bonnet sweeps fluidly to the base of the windscreen. The usual clutter of windscreen wipers, air intakes, and separate scuttle panel has been banished. The front's constantly flowing body skin is interrupted by a vestigial wing necessary to carry the round headlamp of the period. This floating wing style is rather unconventional with only a tenuous link to the car's waistline. To avoid further distraction there's no eyebrow round the simple front wheel cut-out.

In side elevation the sloping bonnet leads to a relatively high windscreen base. The waistline, formed by the bottom of the side glass, then swoops dramatically to the rear bumper. Surprisingly, the rear wheel has no part to play at all in the side view of the body style. Spats or panels covering the rear wheels were relatively common but Bertoni wanted no visual interference in this area. This flush-sided approach, coupled with the teardrop's tapering plan, resulted in the rear wheels being four inches further inboard than the front.

The cabin has original aspects all of its own. The A and B pillars are very thin, this delicate appearance emphasised by frameless side glass and no quarter lights. There is a strong, simple D post panel that makes no attempt to flow into the roof or lower body: all the attention in the rear cabin area is taken by the radically wrapped-around backlight glass. The wrapped-around windscreen and ethereal bright trim on the pillars and cantrail give the impression of a separate, floating roof. The windscreen glass flows seamlessly into the side glass. Again, inspired by the teardrop ethos, the roof is highest at the front, falling with gusto to the rear, visually linking with the bumper. This drives the backlight down, in turn necessitating a dashboard-mounted mirror. The cantrail trims lead to faired-in indicator lamps on the roof's trailing corners; a very late, daring addition.

Not surprisingly such aggressive side and plan elevation taper squeezes the boot area into a rather minor visual role. What little vertical surface is left at the rear of the vehicle carries the remaining quite conventional lamps and number plate.

In 1962 the DS's front apron was slightly refined, increasing top speed by five mph, made possible, no doubt, by the basically clean underbody. Most cars continued to be handicapped by drag-inducing exposed chassis elements. The air dam, discovered in the late 1960s, is used to this day to restrict air under the car if the underside isn't smooth: a compromise the Citroën didn't require.

A drag figure of about .38Cd is usually quoted for the DS. In the 1970s and 80s, when full size wind tunnels began to be used in earnest, an average coefficient of drag was perhaps around .44Cd. In 1982 the Ford Sierra achieved .34Cd, the Audi 100 of the same year, which also majored on aerodynamics, claimed .30Cd.

After the tragic death of Flaminio Bertoni in 1964 Robert Opron became Citroën's chief stylist. From 1963 faired-in headlamps, on smooth new wings, had been considered, presumably influenced by the Panhard 24CT. These were introduced for the 1968 model year. Mock-ups that featured something of a Kamm tail were not adopted. Most usually associated with the DS are the large glass panels that cover the headlamps, but the original solution, even when carrying additional lamps, has its own unique charm.

BODY CONSTRUCTION

Although certainly exotic and *avant-garde*, the DS would have won the approval of Citroën's product engineering team because it lends itself to easy manufacture and assembly.

As a car design student I was lectured on the evils of lead-loading. Lead was commonly used to render invisible the joints between panels: even now there's a limit to how big pressed panels can be made. If a style demanded large unbroken surfaces, filling the inevitable joint with lead solder and working it smooth was the only way to achieve this. This was truly a nightmare for mass production. Operators, for health reasons, literally had to wear spacesuits with complex air filtering systems. Lead can also be unstable in the long term, causing all sorts of problems under the paint finish, including cracking and micro blisters.

The Citroën's panels are quite

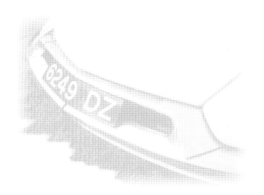

simple: the doors, for instance, don't fit into normal perimeter apertures that invariably cause setting and gapping problems; the drop on the roof is so simple it could be made from a fibreglass moulding. The huge bonnet pressing may have caused alignment problems, but again it didn't have to fit flush into apertures.

Because of the minimal bodywork connection between roof and waistline, dual paint schemes were easy to mask off; Henri Chapron's convertibles look very elegant as the flowing waistline is so strong.

It would be wrong not to mention the tidal wave of legislation that had yet to crash over the automotive industry. Every aspect of a vehicle's exterior/interior, and of course engine emissions is today affected by legislation. In 1955 car design was considerably more straightforward. Crash testing, for instance, now dictates such things as roof pillar thickness, crumple zones, etc. The DS was a pretty good starting point for pending pedestrian impact safety legislation.

STYLING - INTERIOR AESTHETICS

The impact of the DS's interior must have been as dramatic as the exterior. Obviously, the single-spoke steering wheel seemed wilfully, provocatively novel. Perhaps just as challenging was the absence of a conventional dashboard, replaced by a futuristic sweeping, padded, plastic shelf with localised instrument module behind the steering column. There was no gear change, handbrake or transmission tunnel to interrupt the flat floor. Anyone

searching for familiar car-like elements would find only very domestic, soft furnishing-type seats.

With the road wheels pushed away from the cabin, there was not the usual intrusion of inner wheelarches. The genuine feeling of space was further enhanced by the light feel of the delicate glass pillars, which also gave a largely uninterrupted view of the outside world.

Whilst new and highly styled, the interior was essentially practical. For instance, multi-spoke steering wheels give designers problems with field of vision obstruction. The ethereal 'floating rim' approach gave the clearest sight of instruments and controls. Also driven by practicality were the large, featured air vents at the ends of the facia. Bold and novel, they were made necessary by the absence of quarter lights in the side glass. All the facia controls looked and felt delicate, leaning toward the domestic rather than the industrial.

All in all this radical interior echoed the slightly 'not of this world' image of the exterior; the general theme having little or no reference to the machismo or sporty ethos of most car design. As the years passed the DS's facia became more conventional. As every salesman knows, after appraising the exterior the first thing a potential customer does is look through the glass at the dashboard; perhaps it was felt that a more traditional appearance was required ...

THE DS'S CONTEMPORARIES

Turning the pages of a 1955 edition of

the *Observer's Book of Automobiles*, the radical change that the DS represented is most apparent. The only other vehicle similarly influenced by aerodynamics is the Saab 96, also front-wheel drive. Its teardrop-type body ends in a tail not unlike - but less attractive than - the Citroën's. Although fastbacks were not uncommon generally, no other car has the total commitment to a windcheating shape as the DS.

It's necessary to fast forward into the 1960s to really begin to get the Citroën into perspective. At this stage some very interesting styles were emerging: the Jaguar MkII saloons, made famous by bank robbers and Inspector Morse, can stand shoulder to shoulder with the Goddess. The flowing, sculptured surfaces with swooping waistline and low rounded boot are at least as aesthetically pleasing as the Citroën's. The E-type Jaguar - whilst not having to encompass saloon car proportions - also demonstrated how to marry a dynamic thrusting style with soft curves. Notably, of course, the E-type acquired faired-in headlamps in 1961.

Whilst fascinating to pit the Citroën's visual prowess against other cars, this tends to miss the point. Given that at any period in time the engineering constraints on design are pretty much the same for all, the DS has remained in a field of one.

CONCLUSION

Whatever your viewpoint the DS is one of the most interesting cars ever, an incredible combination of technological and aesthetic objectives.

The total vehicle experience was intended to meld engineering and art, two disciplines combined to make the experience of ownership and travel a sensory delight.

Car designers can be ambivalent in their attitude towards the DS's charms. It has to be said that, whilst the car was a landmark design in 1955, it didn't comprehensively lead the way forward. The high-tailed wedge shape, largely pioneered by the 1967 NSU Ro80, more accurately foretold the future. The latter's profile - low nose, low scuttle, raked screen, and high boot - is still the accepted solution for large saloons, giving low aerodynamic drag with high speed stability and maximum luggage space.

It's significant that Citroën acknowledged that the DS didn't fit into the normal architecture or vocabulary of cars. Marketing images exist showing it as a pure form study pointing skyward like an aircraft. Roland Barthes described it as having obviously fallen from the sky, or conversely, as a new Nautilus. Whatever it represented it wasn't your average car.

Designers genuinely didn't know quite how to reconcile this approach with their own vision. Rover chief stylist, David Bache, seems to have tried harder than most: his Rover 2000 of 1963 has been referred to as Britain's DS. Certainly, the whole superstructure above the waist is similar, and there's a familiar feel to the treatment of panel joints and shut lines, both vehicles employing bolt-on body panels. Admired though the Rover is, it never strays beyond the boundaries of conventional styling wisdom, however.

As time passes, and the DS's iconic design status grows, its distinction from modern cars also increases. A truly outrageous by-product of this fresh approach is that the DS's identity is not announced at the front. Traditionally, the frontal area of motor cars has radiator shells, badges, and names with which to project and reinforce product identity: marketing, particularly brand management, has always demanded this and never more so than today. The DS has none: it survived in the market place purely by virtue of its shape.

Another fundamental discrepancy in the Citroën's appearance is the wheel treatment, where there is a lack of visual impact and contribution by the wheels (increasingly the very elements against which the body style is balanced). In the 21st century we have reached a point where huge alloy wheels are the very foundation upon which designs are structured. Again, marketing is able to use this key element to easily differentiate between various models and price levels. Wheels also complement and enhance the generally sporty and powerful image that successful cars project. The DS's wheels are almost irrelevant to the style, and in any case sportiness, and even subtle aggression, is largely absent. This no doubt explains why Citroën marketing was keen to be associated with competition success. Paradoxically, the recent use of faired-in rear wheels on overtly fuel efficient and low emission vehicles may be part of the DS's legacy.

Though the DS's wheels contribute little to the vehicle's presence, its suspension undoubtedly does. Car designers are fascinated by parts of the body moving apparently of their own accord. Historically the Mercedes' air brakes, and nowadays automatic rear spoiler deployment, seem almost robotic. The DS's ability to go from resting on the road to 'getting up' when roused is terrific fun. American customisers spend small fortunes to achieve a similar affect. Designers often struggle to get a vehicle's standing height correct artistically, and ultimately development engineers usually have the final say in the inevitable compromise when using conventional springs.

Given the originality, undoubted presence, and downright intelligence of the DS, one is still forced to pause over its final status in the car world. It would be wrong to suggest that car designers have always universally raved about the car, though, generally, industrial designers and art connoisseurs do.

The *Traction Avant* and, perhaps surprisingly, the Panhard 24CT have always been in my own top ten of cars: probably the Goddess should be also. There is, though, something about the DS that is not quite of the car world. That is not to say that this detracts from it as a piece of design, quite the contrary: I'm just not sure it's playing in the same game as other cars. Because of commercial pressures and desperately high stakes, the 'tear up the rule book' impact of the DS will now remain unique. However, if the Gods ever challenged mankind to produce an artefact as evidence of a desire for betterment, the DS would be a worthwhile candidate.

Graham Hull

Citroën DS

Malcolm Bobbitt

Pallas

INTRODUCTION AND ACKNOWLEDGEMENTS

INTRODUCTION

The Goddess is not a car which can be easily dismissed. Few cars have made as much of an impact on society and the motor industry as this remarkable Citroën - but then, what else would one expect of a manufacturer recognised for its innovative engineering and technology?

Looking at the DS today it's difficult to appreciate that the car's tantalising design is fifty years old, but still as fresh and radical as when it appeared in the autumn of 1955 when unveiled at the Paris Motor Show. There will be people reading this book who were present at the Salon when the wraps hiding Citroën's offering - which, rumour had it, was even more revolutionary than the already technically advanced *Traction Avant* - were removed. They will recall the fervour and excitement as Paris gasped at what was revealed, and the stampede that ensued to place orders for a car that looked like no other.

The DS was more than a revelation: its devastatingly futuristic shape apart, it encompassed technology that was radical in the extreme. Conventionality was consigned to history, as were steel springs, replaced by a system of hydraulics that also provided gear selection and power for braking and steering. It is a cliché to liken the car's styling to that of a spaceship, but in 1955 that is exactly how it looked to visitors to the Salon.

For half a century the DS's pioneering shape has generated debate amongst car designers. The absence of a formal air intake, the curvaceous bonnet line, frameless side windows, roof-mounted indicators, and wings that shroud the rear wheels have combined to intrigue, as well as influence styling trends. There is more, of course: on command the Goddess awakes from her repose, stretches, and glides into the distance without fuss.

Unlike some fifty-year olds the DS conceals her age with graceful sophistication. Those who have succumbed to her charms will agree that she makes a delightful travelling companion; soothing, cosseting, her unique senses refusing to subject her passengers to indifferent ride quality over unsympathetic surfaces. Nor does she allow any compromise in comfort.

The Goddess is symbolic of changing times: arriving at a time when Europe as a whole was emerging from post war austerity, the consequence of such daring design and bristling technology was profound. The car became an icon of growing prosperity and advancing technology: celebrity status was bestowed upon it, and screen and stage idols were keen to pose alongside; it was not difficult to decide who or what possessed the most glamour ... Whoever claimed that the DS was two years ahead of its time was wrong; twenty years after creation, its superiorty was unchallenged.

The DS is a remarkable car with a glorious history, with an enviable reputation for roadholding, comfort and technical wizardry, no better demonstrated than when contending some of the toughest motor sport events. Those who admire the Goddess never tire of her charms; those who

When the DS was introduced in the autumn of 1955 its styling generated much controversy. Fifty years later, Citroën's design is recognised for its outstanding qualities, and is an ageless tribute to those who created it. The car's exterior hides technical innovation that is more advanced than that found on many of today's vehicles. In terms of comfort and driving enjoyment this 1966 DS21 Pallas, which is owned by Charles Vyse, has few, if any, rivals. (Courtesy Charles Vyse)

dismiss her do so because they don't understand the philosophy that went into her design. It's as simple as that!

ACKNOWLEDGEMENTS

I would like to thank the many people who have helped make this book possible. In particular my appreciation goes to Graham Hull, renowned designer and stylist, who readily agreed to share his vast experience of car design in respect of the DS. I am also indebted to Citroën UK, Citroën Paris, Citroën Car Club, Andrew Minney, Brian Drummond, Nigel Wild, Brian Chandler, Joe Judt, Ken Smith, Rodney Cremin, Bill Carrivick, Guy Pursey, Len Drew, Richard Mann, Martin Bourne, Graham Raphael, John White, David Archer, Dave Ashworth, Charles Vyse, David Shepherd, Tony Mather, Tony Stokoe, Brian Scott-Quinn, H John Black, Bill Wolf, Martin Thomas, Andy Burnett, John Reynolds, Dick Lankester, and Sue Magnan. Not least my appreciation goes to my wife, Jean, who for years has endured my enthusiasm for motor vehicles in general and Citroën in particular. A number of images reproduced in this book are from my own collection, which I have amassed over many years. In some cases, the original source is unknown.

Malcolm Bobbitt

Citroën DS

Malcolm Bobbitt

Pallas

The DS in its native France near Angers in 1994. Thirty years or so since the last DS left the factory, the car retains a loyal following and is affectionately regarded, particularly among the French. Around the world the DS is revered for its outstanding contribution to automotive technology. (Author's collection)

CHAPTER ONE

ANDRE CITROËN'S LEGACY

Anyone who has driven on French roads will no doubt have seen that masterpiece of design, the Citroën DS. The car's unmistakable contours make it instantly recognisable, a symbol of radical engineering: only the French could have created something so logical yet so bizarre-looking, which was immediately and unconditionally accepted when introduced in the autumn of 1955.

The descriptions and superlatives applied to the DS are many and varied: spaceship styling, magic carpet ride, poetry in motion, plumber's nightmare, Goddess, and Queen of the *Routes Nationales* spring to mind. Not everyone approves of the car's unique shape or innovative technology, preferring instead rather more conventional design and engineering. Irrespective of personal opinion, an undeniable mystique surrounds the DS; its shape, sumptuous comfort, popularity, technical complexity and, not least, the considerable criticism it has attracted, have all added to its charisma. Whether sweeping gracefully at speed along the poplar-lined roads of northern France, tenaciously negotiating tortuous hairpin bends high above the Mediterranean coast, or sedately gliding through Paris, the DS is completely at home.

Looking at the DS today and appreciating its unique presence it is difficult to believe that fifty or more years have passed since the car made its sensational debut at the Paris Salon. Pronounced 'day-esse', the English translation of which is Goddess, the car's styling remains subtly modern,

courtesy of a superbly aerodynamic shape, which, by comparison with most 1955 designs was and remains, futuristic in the extreme. At the turn of the millennium the DS was voted Product of the Century, ahead of the Boeing 747 Jumbo Jet, Apple Macintosh computer, wind-up radio, and lunar landing module. The DS was also shortlisted as a finalist for the Car of the Century award, an accolade ultimately bestowed on the Model T Ford.

The DS's svelte clothing masks an engineering concept that was, in the

For interior style and armchair comfort the DS knows no equal. This is Charles Vyse's 1966 DS21 Pallas. (Courtesy Charles Vyse)

In 1919 André Citroën (1878-1935) produced the first cars to wear the Double Chevron emblem. Thereafter, he was associated with cars that were robust, innovative, and largely affordable. (Courtesy Citroën)

1950s and '60s, so revolutionary that it established standards of technology by which all other cars for generations to come would be judged. Not present was any conventional form of suspension; coil springs, torsion bars and elliptics having given way to a seemingly complex arrangement of hydraulics that afforded strength and compliancy many times greater than did steel. Additionally, hydraulics provided power assistance for steering and gear selection requiring minimal effort. Braking, too, was dramatically effective and required little application; the lightest pressure on a foot-operated button no larger than an open mushroom would bring the car to a halt with devastating brevity. Last but not least, the braking system used groundbreaking technology inasmuch that front discs, as used on racing Jaguars, were employed for the first time on a production car.

The opulent interior of the DS was unlike that of any other car, and this view is shared by eminent designer, Stephen Bayley, who, writing in *The Daily Telegraph* in 2003, opined that the car's lavishly comfortable seats, akin to armchairs, were vastly superior to those even of a Rolls-Royce limousine, the rear seats inviting passengers to languish in a style hitherto unknown. For the driver and front seat passenger the large curved windscreen and slim roof pillars allowed an uninterrupted view of the road ahead, the car's generous glass area giving excellent all-round visibility. Neither had a car sported before such an aesthetically pleasing console, the radical lines of

which complemented the vehicle's external shape.

Delightful styling touches included deftly-shaped interior furnishings, instrumentation, and fresh air ventilators which perpetuated the DS's adventurous profile. Those visitors to the Paris Salon could be forgiven for thinking that the interior and exterior designs were influenced by the Dan Dare sketches that featured on the front page of *The Eagle*. It would be easy to suggest - and it no doubt has been - that no other car had been fitted with something as simple as a single spoke steering wheel, a device which graced Humber cars before WW1.

For all its futurism the DS was unmistakably of Citroën pedigree. In 1955 when the dust covers were removed at the Paris Salon, André Citroën had been dead for twenty years, but the controversial car that was revealed would surely have delighted Le Patron. A gambler, entrepreneur and industrialist with a penchant for publicity-making endeavours, Citroën had, since 1919 when he unveiled the first car to bear his name, amazed the motoring world with his innovation. His involvement in the motor industry began in 1905 when, aged 27, he supplied 500 engines to the Paris firm of Sizaire-Naudin, maker of reliable motorcars. When André Citroën joined the Mors company in 1908 he increased output of the firm's fine cars, thus turning round its fortunes. We can thank André Citroën for the helical and double helical gear arrangements; although he did not invent them, he perfected their design

and manufacture and accordingly took out a patent in October 1910, having foreseen the potential that was promised. Hence the Double Chevron trademark (representing double helical gears) has appeared, and continues so to do, on all Citroën vehicles.

THE DOUBLE CHEVRON

During the formative years of the 20th century, the use of gearwheels bearing the Citroën patent was widespread, the most famous example being on the steering gear of the ill-fated Titanic. As an engineering student, Citroën was well aware of manufacturing methods that were about to transform America's engineering industry, which would give birth to the expression 'mass production'. Citroën understood the engineering principles that were about to revolutionise the industrial world, and he intended to be at the forefront of the changing technology that would surely encompass Europe.

It was in 1902 that André Citroën established a small engineering workshop near the Gare du Nord in Paris, trading under the name André Citroën & Cie, successfully cutting helical and double helical gears. Three years later in 1905 Citroën expanded his business operation and moved to the Quai de Grenelle, an industrial complex on the left bank of the Seine. Further business development meant that in 1907 he opened sales offices in London, Brussels and Moscow to become a truly international entrepreneur. From premises at Queen Victoria Street in London Citroën marketed his gearwheels, which were

The interior of the Quai de Javel factory in Paris which Citroën built to produce armaments during WW1. The photograph was taken soon after the war when the factory was equipped to manufacture motor vehicles, the Type A being Citroën's first car. (Courtesy Citroën)

highly acclaimed and used throughout British industry in mainly power transmission installations.

When, like all other young Frenchmen (he was born in France and wanted no other nationality, despite his Jewish and Dutch ancestry), he completed his military service, André Citroën became aware that France was ill-equipped for war, such was its reliance on methods used without noticeable change over successive generations. When war was declared in 1914 André Citroën served as a lieutenant in the 2nd Regiment

of Heavy Artillery, a mobilisation which confirmed to him that there existed a serious shortfall in the Army's weaponry and munitions. Industrial firms throughout France were enlisted within regional groups to urgently supply armaments, but the rate at which these were delivered did nothing to

Citroën's name was emblazoned across the Eiffel Tower in Paris between 1924 and 1934, just one of several publicity exercises undertaken by Le Patron. Citroën's name could be seen from a distance of sixty miles at night, courtesy of some 250,000 light bulbs. (Courtesy Citroën)

Citroën's first car, the Type A. Citroën pioneered mass production techniques in Europe and was known as the Henry Ford of France.
(Author's collection)

The double helical gearwheel represented by the Citroën emblem.
(Courtesy Citroën)

reduce the deficit. Owing to the critical situation in which France and its allies found themselves, Citroën - by then promoted to Captain - proposed to the authorities that, with government backing, he could supply some 10,000 shells in a day, a figure in excess of what was currently manufactured by all Paris munitions factories. It was his assurance that he could achieve such an output that won Citroën the contract to produce the all-important munitions, and therefore the means by which to acquire a 30-acre site at the Quai de Javel, on the left bank of the Seine.

Situated 2¼ kilometres from the Eiffel Tower, Citroën's factory, designed from the outset to be self-sufficient in respect of power resources and tooling, was built on open ground that was once market gardens. From the date the land at the Quai de Javel was purchased - 17th March 1915 - it took less than three months to construct the

factory. Daily output of 1500 shells was achieved within two months; less than a month later the figure had risen to 5000 shells a day. By 1917 daily output had reached 15,000; by the time war ended some 23 million shells had been delivered.

The cessation of hostilities meant that Citroën would have to diversify if he was to retain his factory and remain

one of France's premier industrialists. Citroën could easily have adopted any one of several manufacturing enterprises, but arguably the most important - and the one which offered the greatest prospects - was the motor industry. War had shown the motor vehicle's role to be highly significant, not only as a fighting machine but also as an efficient means of transport. In

the wake of the war the motor vehicle's popularity became widespread and no longer was it reserved solely for a select and wealthy clientele. Like Gabriel Voisin in France and W. O. Bentley in Britain, both of whom established themselves as motor manufacturers in 1919, Citroën could well have chosen the luxury market. Notwithstanding that he had already gained valuable experience at Mors, Citroën's instincts instead led him to perpetuate mass production techniques, and to produce a vehicle that was reliable and affordable so would sell in appreciable numbers. When the first Citroën emerged from Javel in 1919 it bore the now famous Double Chevron insignia.

For the first fourteen years Citroën's cars were essentially conventional and conservative in design. Nevertheless, these machines heralded mass production car building techniques in Europe, resulting in André Citroën becoming known as the Henry Ford of France. Robust and competitively priced Citroën's cars certainly were: within the space of a few years they were being constructed in vast numbers that rivalled the

Citroën promoted a number of major geographical expeditions, including the first crossing of the Sahara Desert by motor vehicle, and exploration across Asia traversing the Himalayas. For these missions he used half-track vehicles, an example of which is seen here in central Africa. (Author's collection)

output of Renault, then France's largest constructor of automobiles.

When Citroën first declared that he was to mass produce cars many manufacturers ridiculed the idea, believing such a process to be unworkable. Those who accepted that mass production was indeed possible clearly understood that the repercussions would bring about change in the French motor industry. It was Charles Weiffenbach, Delahaye's managing director, who warned that the small specialist car manufacturers were most at risk from the effects of Citroën's proposal, and that to survive they should form an alliance, but his advice went unheeded. As for Renault and Peugeot, they were large enough to absorb the Citroën shock waves, and in any event had the resources to adopt mass production techniques once it was evident that cars bearing the Double Chevron were seriously influencing French car manufacturing.

CITROËN - ENTREPRENEUR AND PUBLICIST

André Citroën was an opportunist: his had become a household name in France, which was exactly what he had planned. When he hired the Eiffel Tower to emblazon his name high above Paris, courtesy of a quarter of a million light bulbs, visible nearly 100 kilometres away, it was Citroën's illuminated advertisement which greeted pioneer aviator Charles Lindbergh on completion of what was the world's first solo non-stop transatlantic flight in May 1927. Citroën's name is forever associated with a series of geographical expeditions, one of which was when his half-track all-terrain vehicles crossed the Sahara Desert for the first time; similar vehicles ventured into darkest Africa, whilst others traversed the Gobi Desert and the Himalayas, destination Peking.

The 10hp 1327cc Type A was the first Citroën motorcar, which came complete with coachwork and all necessary accessories such as electric lighting and starter, and could be driven away from the showroom, just as car buyers expect today. There was a choice of chassis length, short or normal, and a variety of body styles: tourer; doctor's coupé; saloon, and coupé de ville. Within two years the Type A Special was introduced with a more powerful engine, the 1452cc unit being specified for the Type B2 which superseded the Type A for the 1922 model year. André Citroën also cleverly developed a demure 5hp machine - directed toward lady motorists in particular - which he unveiled at the 1921 Salon. This was a genuine motorcar in miniature and, as such, successfully competed against the many cyclecars in existence. By the middle of 1926 this delightful manifestation of minimal motoring, of which nearly 90,000 examples were produced, was discontinued. Ironically a hungry appetite remained for such a no-frills economy car, a market satisfied by Herbert Austin's little miracle, the Austin Seven.

When the B10 replaced the B2 for the 1925 model year, André Citroën showed the way forward by promoting the *tout acier* (all-steel) bodyshell developed by the Budd Corporation of Philadelphia in America. Then came the B12 with its stronger chassis and use of front wheel brakes (ironically, Citroën was behind Renault and Peugeot in introducing front wheel braking). This model remained in production for one year before being replaced by the B14 with its 1539cc engine and vacuum servo brakes.

In 1928 Citroën introduced a range of six-cylinder cars which were noted for their performance and comfort. This example is pictured in Paris in 1991. (Author's collection)

In 1928 the Citroën range was dramatically expanded when the 'AC' (referring to Le Patron's name) series of cars was launched, there being a six-cylinder variant in addition to a four-cylinder. Six-cylinder models were achieving greater popularity and, as a result, were being offered by increasing numbers of motor manufacturers to satisfy customer demand. The increased power and smoothness of operation that six-cylinder engines afforded prompted firms, including Citroën, to introduce cars with heavier and more commodious coachwork. A greater variety of body styles was offered, often courtesy of bespoke coachbuilders,

Nicolas and Sical amongst others.

When Citroën became involved in a series of endurance feats in association with the Yacco oil company during the early 1930s, the family of cars that made history at the Montlhéry track outside Paris became known as *Les Petites Rosalies*. The record attempts caught the imagination of the French people, and in fact the *Rosalie* appellation was coined from a song that was popular at the time. Three models were representative of the *Rosalie* theme; the 8 and 10CV, both four-cylinder cars, and the six-cylinder 15CV. For the first time Citroëns had the Double Chevron insignia festooned across their radiator grilles instead of confined to the top of the radiator shell in the shape of an enamelled motif. Racing driver Cesar Marchand, a veteran of Montlhéry driving mainly Voisins, was enlisted to put the *Rosalie*, which was fitted

with a streamlined body, through its paces. For 134 days in 1933 Marchand maintained momentum, completing nearly 200,000 miles (320,000 kms) to average 57.8mph and break numerous records which went unchallenged for many years.

André Citroën had not previously contemplated entering motorsport events for the reason that his cars were not designed to compete with those machines dominating Le Mans, Montlhéry, and elsewhere. Not in the league of Alfa Romeo, Delage, Delahaye, Talbot or Bentley, they nonetheless promised efficient and relatively inexpensive transport for thousands of motorists in France and around the world. Citroëns were, however, well suited to endurance trials, in events such as the Monte Carlo Rally, which were popular with motorists in general.

During the early 1930s Citroën involved himself in a series of endurance attempts at Montlhéry on the outskirts of Paris. Racing driver Cesar Marchand completed nearly 200,000 miles in 134 days, averaging 57.8mph in a Citroën Rosalie and establishing records which remained unbroken for many years. (Author's collection)

In France Citroën had become general provider: as well as operating a network of taxi cabs in all the big cities, the company controlled a national coach service, its fleet of vehicles providing comfortable and regular transport throughout the country. Citroën dominated the commercial market; seen everywhere, the Double Chevron vehicles undertook a multitude of roles such as delivery van, pick-up, tractor unit, breakdown truck, ambulance, hearse, fire tender, and more. Citroën was also at the forefront of diesel engine technology, and it was he, in association with Sir Harry Ricardo, who developed the first diesel-engined car.

DRIVING FORWARD

The DS's dramatic appearance in 1955 evoked memories of the birth of Citroën's first front-wheel drive car, the *Traction Avant*, twenty-one years earlier in May 1934. That, too, was an occasion to be remembered, as André Citroën unveiled his sleek and streamlined saloon that boasted so many radical features, all of which were known about but never before seen together on a

When Citroën unveiled his Traction Avant *in 1934 it was considered very radical with its front-wheel drive, all-round torsion bar suspension, monocoque bodyshell and hydraulic brakes. Seen here with Le Patron is François Lecot who, for a wager, drove his* Traction Avant *250,000 miles in 369 days. (Courtesy Citroën)*

mass produced vehicle. The *Traction Avant* was André Citroën's pinnacle of achievement, the car's low centre of gravity, coupled with its chassis-less construction, torsion bar suspension and hydraulic braking ensured it stood apart from all others. Now recognised as a landmark blueprint, the *Traction Avant* influenced automotive design for several decades, including the car's successor, the DS.

The *Traction* had exceptional road holding, and without doubt driving one of these cars in 1934 must have been a unique experience. The car's low centre

of gravity combined with front-wheel drive meant that it could cope with driving conditions that vehicles with narrow track and tall bodies would have found impossible. A favourite ploy of Citroën salesmen, demonstrating the *Traction* to potential customers, was to drive it on and off pavements to demonstrate its stability.

André Citroën conceived the idea of developing the *Traction Avant* in the wake of the economic depression which wreaked havoc around the world. At the end of the 1920s, Automobiles Citroën was responsible for forty per cent of France's motor vehicle output, a market share that fell to below thirty per cent within three years. Le Patron accepted that if he was to regain lost ground he had to introduce a machine that was so advanced in design it would give his company a substantial technological lead, especially in respect of his rival, Louis Renault, whose massive motor works dominated the opposite bank of the Seine at Billancourt.

Citroën knew exactly what he wanted. In 1931 a design, still top secret, had been shown to him

whilst on one of his visits to the Budd Corporation. Seeing what Budd had to offer he instantly realised that the concept would revolutionise automotive technology sufficiently to put him leagues ahead of his rivals. The design that Citroën had seen was quite different to anything else then available, having materialised from the fertile minds of Joseph Ledwinka and William J. Muller: by incorporating chassis and body as a monocoque and employing front-wheel drive, it was possible to achieve a low centre of gravity and stability hitherto unknown. There was more: without the hindrance of a separate heavy chassis frame it was possible to design a superbly streamlined body that accommodated four or five people in complete comfort within an extremely modestly sized passenger compartment. Citroën understood that such a radical design would have to be carefully developed if it were to win acceptance, and as long as this could be achieved it would give him at least a five year lead over his rivals. Not even the perceptive Citroën could have anticipated that

the car would enjoy a production life of twenty-three years, and even afterward still be considered more advanced than many designs then in production.

Having decided that the front-wheel drive car with its unitary construction offered him the development project that he so badly needed, André Citroën lost no time consolidating his efforts. Unlike the cautious Louis Renault, Citroën was less pragmatic: living his life as if it was a gamble, it had been known for him to risk his livelihood, and that of others, by wagering his company on a hand of cards at the poker table. Whether he could actually afford the cost of developing the new car mattered not, despite what would be an enormous and virtually open-ended investment.

The embryonic *Traction Avant* was given the code name *Petite Voiture* which was shortened to simply 'PV'. Initial development was carried out in Paris in complete anonymity away from the Javel factory in the Rue du Théâtre, premises which once belonged to the Mors company. There Citroën assembled a team of designers and engineers which included Raoul Cuinet, Pierre Franchiset (who was also involved with the DS), and Jean Daninos, the trio having responsibility for designing the bodyshell as proposed by the Budd Corporation. The styling of the car, its bodyshell and interior, was entrusted to Italian Flaminio Bertoni; Maurice Julien took control of the suspension whilst Maurice Sainturat was charged with engine design. In overall charge was Maurice Broglie, Citroën's chief engineer, who had the task of complying with Le Patron's incessant demands.

The undertaking presented to this select team was, understandably, colossal, and not without many problems. Front-wheel drive had been used to good effect on a number of marques, including Adler, Alvis, Cord, DKW, Ruxton, and Tracta. Unitary construction had also been used previously, but only in a few specialist instances. Employing both features together was new, and especially so on a design to be mass produced. Entirely new theories had to be examined and understood, all of which went well beyond developing a known arrangement, and a degree of scepticism was felt by most dedicated engineers. Le Patron was, nevertheless, insistent that the PV should encompass the most far-reaching technology, and this included developing automatic transmission. To achieve this Citroën appointed inventor Dimitri Sensaud de Lavaud to engineer an infinitely variable transmission system, a version of which had already been used by Gabriel Voisin on his magnificent sports cars.

It was Gabriel Voisin whom Citroën approached when he needed particular expertise in developing some of the finer aspects of the PV's design. Citroën and Voisin were old friends, Citroën having anticipated buying the proceeds of Voisin's luxury car manufacturing business (Voisins were often referred to as the French equivalent of Bentleys) when economic depression forced him to cease manufacture. Voisin, noted for his innovative engineering, had no hesitation in recommending André Lefebvre, a young but brilliant engineer whose career included racing Voisins. Lefebvre had worked for Voisin, ironically on a proposed front-wheel drive car, but after the firm's collapse had sought a position with Renault. For Lefebvre, his tenure at Billancourt was a disaster, the conservative manufacture constantly spurning the young designer's innovative ideas.

It was to their mutual benefit that Lefebvre went to work for Citroën. At Javel the young engineer could progress his radical ideas with Le

When the Traction Avant *was introduced in 1934 it was driven by a 1303cc engine. Underpowered, it was soon fitted with larger engines, the most popular being the 1911cc ohv unit which, in modified form, also powered the DS. (Author's collection)*

Patron's full authority. Such was Lefebvre's expertise and understanding of Citroën's forward-thinking principles that he was promoted to overall control of *Traction Avant* development in time for the car's proposed launch in the spring of 1934. Lefebvre had exactly a year in which to overcome many technical problems ...

TIGHT SCHEDULE

The timescale allowed for the *Traction's* development was so tight as to be virtually impossible to achieve. Accepting that Le Patron refused to be persuaded to allow more time for the project's development, Lefebvre and his team of engineers worked around the clock, firstly identifying design problems and then establishing remedies. Within three months Lefebvre had a prototype car ready for testing, the design meeting with Citroën's rigorous demands.

There were several reasons for Le Patron's impatience: a new and radical car would earn for him much needed revenue, essential if he was to recoup the cost of major refurbishment of the Javel factory, an exercise embarked upon by Citroën to rival Louis Renault's expansion at Billancourt. Citroën's financial resources, which had often been shaky, were now critical, a situation exacerbated by a downturn in business in addition to soaring costs associated with the *Traction Avant's* development. There was also the question of André Citroën's credibility; news had leaked that he was about to introduce a radical new car, and delays would harm his image. Not

least, rumours were circulating about Le Patron's health; stomach cancer had been diagnosed.

Problem after problem threatened the *Traction's* scheduled introduction, but still Le Patron refused to allow his engineers more time. It was only when Sensaud de Lavaud's automatic transmission proved unreliable on a prototype car (it had worked well when fitted to a *Rosalie*) that Lefebvre finally convinced Citroën to agree to fit a conventional clutch and three-speed gearbox ahead of the engine and abandon Sensaud de Lavaud's arrangement.

Unconventional, however, was the gear selection mechanism, which culminated in what has since become known as the 'mustard spoon' sprouting from the facia. There were problems with driveshaft design, the Gregoire type having to be replaced by one with constant velocity joints devised by Glaenzer. There remained many other

difficulties, not least of which was that bodyshells on pre-production cars were showing symptoms of acute stress, and on occasions actually splitting apart.

The pressure on Lefebvre to rectify all of the *Traction's* teething troubles was enormous. Despite Lefebvre's pleas Le Patron adamantly refused to delay the car's launch, which meant that when it was unveiled to leading Citroën concessionaires on 24th March 1934 - to universal acclaim, of course, - the *Traction* was not ready to enter production. The 7A, as it was known, was introduced to the media in mid-April, and a month later was on general sale at the same price as a *Rosalie*. Despite press adoration, the 7A was, in reality, a sorry mess. Customers experienced a myriad of problems with the car's brakes, suspension and transmission, all of which were addressed by Citroën dealerships following endeavours by Lefebvre and his overworked team.

When the Paris Salon opened

on 3rd October 1934 visitors were treated to an all-encompassing range of Citroën's front-wheel drive models which included a wealth of body and engine arrangements. The original 7A, with its dreadfully underpowered 1303cc engine, was replaced by a series of cars featuring four engine configurations, three of which were the 1529cc 7B, the higher performance 1628cc 7C, and the 1911cc 11, the latter remaining throughout the life of the *Traction* and beyond into the DS era. In developed form, the engine remained in production until 1981, by which time the CX had superseded the DS, thus ending the remarkable career of an exceptional piece of engineering.

The fourth engine was in the form of a 3.8 litre V8, sufficient to effortlessly propel Citroën's super-*Traction*, the 22, to 140km/h. It is said that Le Patron had been so highly impressed with Ford's V8 that he ordered his designers to prepare a car that would rival and surpass it. The 22 never went into production owing to too many technical difficulties, not least of which was that total effort was directed at rectifying problems with the four-cylinder cars. Had the 22 materialised beyond prototype form, it would have been a masterpiece of design and engineering, road testing having indicated quiet running with unbelievable acceleration. Development of the car was finally curtailed by Citroën's spectacular financial collapse.

FALL OF AN EMPIRE

The fragile state of Citroën's finances was no secret. The firm's creditors, the largest of which was Michelin, were generally sympathetic, recognising that introduction of the *Traction Avant* promised recovery of the massive investment that had been necessary for the car's development. When a relatively minor creditor took legal action it had the effect of dramatically toppling one of France's best known and most productive companies. Declared insolvent, André Citroën's empire fell to Michelin which, with its huge resources, was able to install a programme to perfect the design of the *Traction* within weeks, the revenue

The old and the new ... A Citroën DS23 Pallas leading a convoy of Traction Avant*s at Glamis Castle in 2003. (Author's collection)*

The Traction Avant *celebrated its 70th anniversary in 2004 with some 1000 cars attending a special event at Dunkerque. The prewar car is identified as such by the two opening ports each side of the bonnet. (Author's collection)*

The Traction Avant *found many customers around the world, including Shotaro Kobayashi pictured with his right-hand drive car during a Japanese winter.* (Author's collection)

from the model recovering all of Citroën's liabilities within two years.

The stress of the months leading to the *Traction's* debut, the legal action and subsequent loss of his empire, was too much for André Citroën to endure. Already ill and significantly weakened by these events, he succumbed to stomach cancer and died on July 3rd 1935 at the age of 56.

With the *Traction Avant* setting new standards of automotive design following its inauspicious start, proposals to eventually replace it were formulated in 1938 by Pierre Boulanger, the engineer Michelin had installed as Citroën's managing director. Boulanger wanted the car ready for 1940, a development programme that would have been highly optimistic to say the least. Entrusting the design work to the very capable Lefebvre, and the styling to Bertoni, advance applications progressed around a notion that was adventurous even by Citroën standards. Ultimately, this was confined to streamlining the *Traction* to enhance styling themes emerging from some of Europe's most progressive motor architects.

The onset of war in 1939 put a hold on further development, and by the time Lefebvre and Bertoni were able to return to their deliberations they had reassessed their objectives. The *Traction's* replacement was to be a design far more radical than was originally conceived, both in terms of styling and engineering.

Citroën DS

Malcolm Bobbitt

Chapter Two

GENESIS OF A CONCEPT

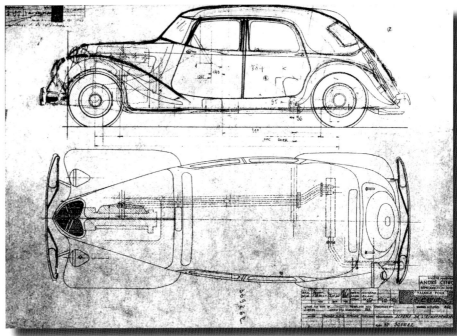

In 1939 a page from Flaminio Bertoni's sketchpad depicts his initial ideas for the Traction Avant's successor, showing how the *Traction's outline can be smoothed and streamlined. It's interesting to see how Bertoni adopted a 'fastback' style of coachwork, in keeping with some of the more progressive styling to emerge during the closing years of that decade. (Courtesy Citroën)*

Had Pierre Boulanger's anticipated timetable for the *Traction Avant's* replacement not been interrupted by war, Citroën evolution could quite easily have taken a very different course. The image that evolved on Flaminio Bertoni's sketch pad in 1939 displayed characteristics that were essentially *Traction Avant* in nature, the familiar outline plainly evident in the bodyshell and roofline arrangements despite some streamlining.

Overall, Bertoni's draft reflected a softening of an already aesthetic design, the stylist's ideas for the car's frontal aspect being most specific. Here, he dramatically applied the principle of aerodynamics to streamline the radiator shell and incorporate headlamps into front wings reshaped to give a distinct wheelarch. Bertoni's styling statement resurged in his early post war sketches

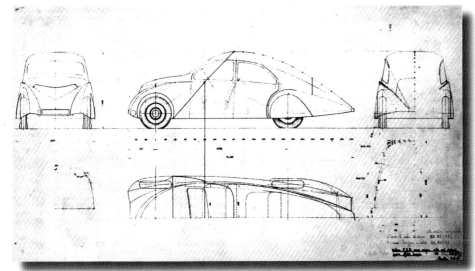

*Bertoni's styling ideas for Project VGD (*Voiture à Grande Diffusion*) dated 1939. Had the onset of war not intervened, a successor to the Traction Avant could well have been announced at the end of 1940. In contrast to the above diagram it can be seen how Bertoni's arrangement had matured. (Courtesy Citroën)*

when he and André Lefebvre were able to return to defining the model's replacement.

With production of the *Traction Avant* successfully under way after a faltering start, and early problems with the car satisfactorily remedied, the *Bureau d'Etudes*, Citroën's design department, settled down to pursue a number of innovative ideas. In addition to preparing a design that would ultimately replace the *Traction*, much work was carried out devising an ultra-utilitarian machine, the prototype of which was ready for testing before the onset of war. Post war this emerged as the 2CV, a landmark design characterised by its nose-down attitude and corrugated appearance courtesy of Lefebvre and Bertoni working under Boulanger's direction. Like the VW Beetle, Renault's 4CV, Fiat Cinquecento and the Morris Minor, Citroën's minimalist tin snail provided affordable motoring in a period of post war austerity.

The period at Javel immediately before WW2 and during hostilities was one of intense development. Along with the 2CV assignment and work to replace the *Traction Avant*, development progressed on a series of commercial projects which materialised as the forward control TUB van in 1939, forerunner to the idiosyncratic but nevertheless highly versatile H van introduced in 1947. The foregoing may seem obscure in relation to DS development, but the

formidable team that headed Citroën's design work. Pierre Boulanger's vision for the *Traction Avant's* replacement was adventurous, but not nearly so audacious as André Lefebvre might have wished. Gabriel Voisin's influence was instilled in Lefebvre, and he yearned to produce a car that was truly radical. Few would disagree that Lefebvre more than anyone else was responsible for maintaining the Citroën philosophy following Le Patron's death, and he guided the *Bureau d'Etudes* through its most innovative era. Had not Lefebvre suffered a severe stroke in his early sixties, leaving him partially paralysed and causing him to retire in 1958, there's no guessing what groundbreaking ideas might have materialised from his team of design engineers.

Before the war Pierre Boulanger had laid down specific parameters for the *Traction's* replacement: known as the Voiture à Grande Diffusion - hence the project code name VGD - the new initiative was expected to be two models; one capable of attaining a speed of 125km/h, the other 135km/h, thus acquiring VGD125 and VGD135 nomenclature. Speeds of 78mph and 84mph respectively were highly optimistic for the vast majority of production saloon cars of the era, and certainly faster than the *Traction Avant* could safely maintain and still provide absolute comfort for occupants. Boulanger's aspirations were far-reaching: he foresaw a machine that gave ultimate comfort, and to achieve this he anticipated that an innovatory approach towards

case for its inclusion becomes clear when explained by Ken Smith, chief engineer at Citroën's British factory in Slough.

Ken Smith recalls that Paul Magès, Citroën's specialist on suspension and braking systems, began to study an application of load-sensitive braking for the then current TUB van, but his work was inconclusive. Magès then experimented with a system that was fitted to the PUD7 commercial vehicle in 1942, this having a mechanical

load-sensing linkage at the rear axle. When this application also proved unconvincing Magès looked elsewhere for a solution, and decided that the use of hydraulic fluid under high pressure offered the best direction. Ken recognises that Magès's work was the true genesis of the Citroën hydropneumatic system, and paved the way for its use in other functions of the motor vehicle.

When work at the *Bureau d'Etudes* resumed after the war it was a

In addition to the VGD project, work was carried out simultaneously at Javel on a number of other assignments, not least of which concerned a series of commercial vehicles. During 1939, and throughout the early war years, exercises were conducted on a prototype forward control van using load-sensitive braking. Engineer, Paul Magès, experimented with hydraulics, and the result of his work was the true genesis of Citroën's hydropneumatic system. The prototype commercial vehicle, known as the TUB, emerged in post war years as the ubiquitous H Van. (Author's collection)

suspension technology would be required. The then notoriously poor state of French roads meant that much had to be accomplished if a car's occupants were to be insulated from surfaces that were often appalling by British standards. There was much more of course, as to achieve the speeds envisaged by Boulanger it was necessary to study the fundamentals of vehicle construction in order to keep weight to a minimum; additionally, any design had to be aerodynamically perfect.

Pierre Boulanger was emphatic that in order for Lefebvre and his team to arrive at a suitable blueprint for the VGD nothing was to be ignored or forsaken, however radical or revolutionary it might seem. Even at that time the concept of designing a lightweight platform, tubular-built from either steel or aluminium, to which panels could be attached, was not dismissed. Bertoni's early styling

themes, and those he resumed after the war, reflect the secret proposals being considered at the *Bureau d'Etudes*.

A NEW BEGINNING
During the war years the cessation of car production generated much discussion in the motoring press about automotive styling in general, retrospectively as well as forecasting future trends. Styling themes predicted by the motor industry's most respected commentators were carefully noted, and Britain's principal motoring journals, *The Autocar* and *The Motor*, indicated that previously upright designs, often featuring razor-edge

styling, were being replaced by subtle curves. By incorporating wings with a sloping bonnet, a full-width styling effect could be achieved along with smaller air intakes.

Lefebvre was far in advance of such discussion, his idea being to completely eliminate the conventional air intake by devising a frontal shape that would have a drag-coefficient as low as possible. Intake of air for engine cooling purposes, he considered, could be achieved by designing a scoop beneath and behind the bumper without compromising air resistance.

Such a styling configuration had evolved through Lefebvre's belief that a teardrop was aerodynamically perfect in shape, a formula Bertoni had incorporated to produce a rounded nose and tapering roof and tail. Lefebvre was not alone in his ideals, the subject of streamlining having been studied by various stylists, coachbuilders and manufacturers, with designs as diverse as Figoni et Falaschi's arrangements

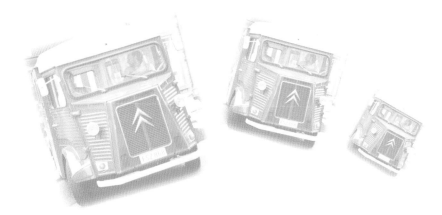

for Talbot-Lago and Bugatti, Sir Charles Dennistoun Burney's Streamline, Georges Paulin's Pourtout-built Bentley, Hans Ledwinka's Tatra and, post war, the Bristol, and Bentley R-Type Continental. There were other developments, but few were as significant as that undertaken by Panhard which culminated in the unveiling of the Dynavia concept car at the 1949 Brussels Motor Show. This was the epitome of the teardrop shape so envisaged by Lefebvre and, in this instance, was designed by Louis Bionier who, like his counterpart at Javel, looked to aircraft fuselage configuration as the basis for future motorcar design.

Rather than allow the VGD concept to evolve simply as a re-styled *Traction Avant*, André Lefebvre was determined to incorporate the work with hydraulics and hydropneumatics that Paul Magès had conducted, since this appealed to his strong sense of individuality. Whether Pierre Boulanger fully approved of Lefebvre's radical approach to the VGD project, which brought about the DS, will never be known. In 1950, whilst driving a *Traction Avant* fitted with an experimental engine and transmission at speed along the Route Nationale 7 near Clermont-Ferrand, the car inexplicably left the road and struck a tree, killing Boulanger outright. It is known that Boulanger was toying with an idea to replace the 15-6, Citroën's six-cylinder 2.8 litre car, with something rather more powerful, 3½ and 4½ litre models having been proposed. The cause of the accident, which has remained a mystery, left the

VGD project in some doubt. Moreover, Citroën's innovative culture might well have been in jeopardy had not Boulanger's successor, Robert Puiseux, upheld the work of his predecessor and especially that of Lefebvre and his dedicated design team.

History has revealed that Boulanger's untimely death instigated massive stimulation within the Bureau d'Etudes. Under Puiseux's direction, and headed by Pierre Bercot, work on the VGD campaign accelerated notably, much of the formative work having come to fruition around the time of Boulanger's death to allow the project to move forward quickly. Shortly before he died Boulanger had been anxious about getting the design finalised: experimental work on suspension systems had shown that a high pressure hydropneumatic arrangement was fundamentally better than a low pressure type, and that work undertaken on an air-cooled flat-six engine configuration was not progressing as well as had been hoped.

On taking over the work that his predecessor had initiated, Robert Puiseux's acknowledgement of Boulanger's direction, and his confidence in Lefebvre's vision to produce for Citroën the car of the future, acted as a fillip to personnel within the *Bureau d'Etudes*. In the early 1950s, therefore, Lefebvre's team had reached a critical stage. Experiments with a high pressure hydropneumatic suspension system had proved successful; styling had progressed to a stage where full-scale mock-ups were

a reality and emerging engine designs were looking promising, despite there being much development work still to be done.

Engine design was the responsibility of Walter Becchia, an Italian engineer whose foray into the automotive industry came courtesy of Fiat's racing department. In 1923 he left Italy for Wolverhampton, having been recruited by Louis Coatalen, Sunbeam's enigmatic chief designer who collaborated with W. O. Bentley on aero engine design during WW1. There Becchia worked under Coatalen's direction to devise the 2 litre six-cylinder engine that powered Henry Segrave's Sunbeam to victory in the 1923 French Grand Prix, the first time Britain had won this prestigious event. Becchia departed Sunbeam in 1926 to work in France for Talbot-Darracq, a position which led him to undertake engine design for Talbot-Lago, whose cars swept the board at the 1937 French Grand Prix at Montlhéry. In recognising Becchia's talents, Pierre Boulanger invited him to move to Citroën in 1941 where he worked alongside his compatriot Flaminio Bertoni. At Javel Becchia created his horizontally-opposed, air-cooled, twin-cylinder engine, a masterpiece of engineering which propelled nearly seven million 2CVs.

Like Bertoni, Becchia revelled in producing innovative designs, his proposal for the VGD's engine reflecting in no small way his inventive approach to engineering. Experience acquired in designing the 2CV engine encouraged Becchia to opt for an air-cooled flat-

During prewar years work at Javel was given over to designing what was to become the 2CV, with its air-cooled flat-twin engine. Walter Becchia was assigned the 2CV's engine design and was later appointed to design an engine for the proposed DS. This early example of a 2CV was pictured in August 2003 at London's Design Museum which hosted an exhibition devoted to Flaminio Bertoni's work for Citroën. Among the cars that Bertoni styled were the Traction Avant, Ami 6, and DS. (Author's collection)

six configuration. In addition to it being extremely compact he believed it would offer optimum performance coupled with minimal maintenance requirements.

Becchia's engine was a single camshaft all-alloy affair with push-rod operated valves, air-cooled by a fan which forced air through ducts across the cylinders. Extensive testing showed there to be problems with cooling the middle cylinders, which prompted

A 2CV as depicted in the BBC television series Maigret, screened in 1961. Inspector Maigret was played by the late Rupert Davies, an avid Citroën enthusiast. (Courtesy BBC)

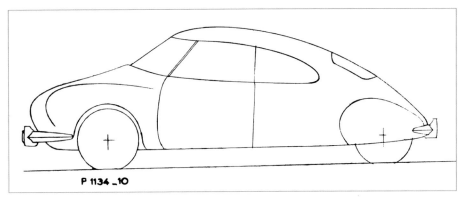

Following his earlier sketches for Project VGD, Bertoni changed to a sleeker, more aerodynamic approach, the profile illustrated here dating from the 1940s. The definitive DS shape is evident. (Courtesy Citroën)

Becchia to re-appraise his design and re-examine earlier experiments by Gabriel Voisin with a prototype 2CV engine. Like Voisin, Becchia enclosed the cylinder heads with a shroud so that the air, heated as it passed over the finned cylinders, was extracted, together with exhaust gas emissions.

Though Becchia largely overcame the difficulties with engine cooling, his design had yet to undergo extensive testing. Rather than rely on air-cooling, which had proved reliable and efficient on the 375cc 2CV, Lefebvre instructed Becchia to devise a water-cooled flat-six which, in order to comply with Bertoni's styling of a low bonnet line, called for the radiator to be positioned behind the engine. Problems attributed to water circulation were apparent from the outset, the most acute causing a bank of cylinders to intermittently misfire. A much more fundamental problem arose when prototype testing began. Atrocious handling characteristics were experienced, the result of the flat-six engine with gearbox in tandem being placed ahead of the front wheels in such a forward position that it was necessary to accommodate the leading pair of cylinders beneath prominent bulges in the bonnet. Photographic evidence of the prototype vehicle is limited to a single poor quality image of a car with a circular air intake at the base of its deeply contoured bonnet, a curved divided windscreen, and a fabric roof.

Enraged by the delay to overall development of the VGD project

that continuing problems caused, Lefebvre called for a total re-appraisal of engine design, prompting serious disagreement between himself and Walter Becchia. Contemporary reports suggest that the atmosphere within the *Bureau d'Etudes* was heavy with animosity; Becchia insisted that had he been allowed to properly develop the flat-six, whether air- or water-cooled, it would have been a realistic alternative to conventional engine design.

Elsewhere in France Jean-Albert Grégoire had already designed his front-wheel drive Aluminium Français-Grégoire (AFG) with its flat-twin engine. The design was ultimately adopted by Panhard to become that company's Dyna models. There was also Grégoire's technically advanced flat-four 2-litre which made its debut at the 1947 Paris Salon, whilst in Britain the Bradford firm of Jowett was also an exponent of the horizontally-opposed engine, and the Javelin, with its all-torsion-bar suspension, received high acclaim. While little need be said about Volkswagen's legendary air-cooled flat-four Beetle, Citroën, ironically, did not progress multi-cylinder air-cooling until introduction of the highly innovative 4-cylinder 1015cc GS model in the early seventies.

It was Lefebvre's decision, with Puiseux's backing, that further thoughts of a horizontally-opposed engine be abandoned in favour of specifying the *Traction Avant's* 2-litre engine, albeit in slightly revised form. In adopting the *Traction's* four-cylinder engine, work on the VGD project had effectively to take a new direction, thus calling for

a complete overhaul of design and styling arrangements.

André Lefebvre's decision to re-appraise the VGD project was undoubtedly the cause of much consternation within the *Bureau d'Etudes*. Flaminio Bertoni's early post war studies for the VGD theme had evolved to a point where the definitive DS image was clearly exemplified, his renderings characterising the familiar scuttle, front wings and low swage line. Had that design, which received the somewhat unfortunate *l'hippopotame* (hippopotamus) appellation, emerged as the production DS, it would have been sufficiently radical, with its bonnet and wings forming a massive single unit, to generate huge controversy. The rear of the car, comprising tail, screen and wings that supported enclosed wheelarches, was similarly constructed, but overtones of the *Traction Avant* remained inasmuch that the front doors were the rear-hinged 'suicide' type. Not typical of the *Traction*, however, was the use of curved windscreen glass front and rear, such technology then in its infancy although Chrysler had used curved glass for its Airflow model in 1934.

The styling of *l'hippopotame* caused Bertoni some disquiet for he completed several designs, all of which depicted differing suggestions of tail arrangement. Formative sketches depicted a bustle tail, later supplanted by a 'fastback' arrangement similar to that favoured by American stylists in the late 1940s, and which graced Peugeot's 203 model when shown at the Paris Salon in 1948. While Bertoni's

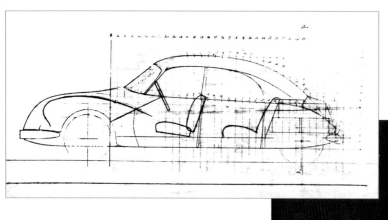

Bertoni chose to modify the fastback design to incorporate a bustle … (Courtesy Citroën)

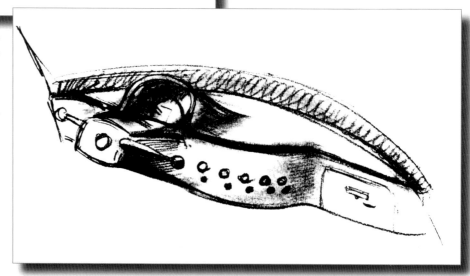

… which is shown here with greater clarity. Bertoni's drawing dates from the late 1940s, his design becoming known as l'hippopotame (hippopotamus). Note the definition of the bonnet, front wings and swage line. (Courtesy Citroën)

sketches were totally appealing, the clay scale models, known as *maquettes*, appeared all the more extreme, especially with Double Chevrons prominently displayed on their nose cones.

Mention has been made of Louis Bionier's design for Panhard which emerged in the late 1940s as the Dynavia. Few images exist of this aerodynamic offering with its near-perfect teardrop shape, but when a prototype example was pictured at Orléans in 1948, its profile was deemed remarkably similar to Bertoni's design ideas of the same period.

Above & right: In addition to radical exterior styling, Bertoni considered some innovative ideas for the car's interior, these two illustrations depicting a dashboard quite alien to anything in production. Note that the stylist was at one time doing away with the conventional steering wheel in preference to a handlebar arrangement. (Courtesy Citroën)

Complying with Lefebvre's instructions to utilise the *Traction's* reliable if somewhat agricultural engine meant some deft restyling by Bertoni in order to achieve the aerodynamic shape that Lefebvre desired. Instead of mounting the engine forward with the gearbox behind, it was necessary to return to the formula used for the *Traction*: placing the motor further back within the engine compartment and installing the gearbox ahead of it. For Bertoni to adopt a bonnet line that rose gently from the bumper to form a relatively high-mounted scuttle, a necessary manoeuvre if the engine was to be successfully accommodated beneath it, the engine had to be set so far back that it intruded into the passenger cabin. Here, at last, was the definitive DS frontal profile complete with smooth underside and high-set headlamps built into the leading edges of the wings. In attempting to maintain the teardrop shape that he had evolved in the late forties, Bertoni favoured a steeply raked convex windscreen, the upper edge of which abutted the slim roof, which swept downward to form a sharply pointed tail.

The rear wings also had the definitive form, though clearly Bertoni wavered about totally enclosing the rear wheelarches. Several attempts were made to re-assert the rear profile as a whole, not only to provide a rear screen

that gave good visibility, but also to give a roofline which allowed optimum headroom for rear seat passengers. It was now 1954 and Bertoni had had time to reflect on current styling trends. Six-light configurations were becoming popular, and glass areas were being enlarged, which prompted Bertoni to raise the roofline to provide for a third window each side of the car as well as affording more interior space. More importantly, Bertoni was able to achieve the fast-back shape that Lefebvre so admired.

This, then, appeared to be the ultimate design, Citroën management having sanctioned its approval in the autumn of 1954. For Lefebvre and his team the time had come to embark on the next project: design a convertible version of the VGD.

When Bertoni decided on some significant last minute restyling, it caused panic in the *Bureau d'Etudes*, leading to abandonment of the VGD convertible project. News that Simca had acquired the interests of Ford France, effective from November 1954, and that a new car was to be introduced at the 1954 Paris Salon, was sufficient to alert Citroën management. Simca's arrangement allowed it to break into a more expensive market, from which Citroën, Renault, and Peugeot currently profited.

With the Ford deal came a modern

factory at Poissy where all Simca production would be undertaken. Simca's plans for the 2355cc litre V8 Vedette to be built as three models - one basically equipped, another a mid-range car, and a luxury alternative - became all the more important. Though details were sketchy it was evident that the Vedette, with its radical styling, might seriously compromise the success of the VGD. Ford's new model promised to dispense with the soft styling previously seen on the Simca Aronde models, and introduce to Europe angular lines and, eventually, large rear fins which were popular features on American cars. Bertoni feared that American fashions would make European cars - with their more curvaceous shapes - look seriously dated. What happened, of course, was that the American idiom of using acres of chrome and large fins was shortlived.

Ken Smith - in early 1955 working with engineers at the Paris factory - recalls that Citroën management also made it known that a German manufacturer was intending to launch a car of similar image to the VGD, including a continuous roofline that swept down to the rear bumper. The only car to sport such styling was the 896cc, 3-cylinder, two-stroke DKW, which, in reality, was no threat to Citroën, even though in excess of

Only months from introduction, design changes resulted in a new rear profile for the DS. This drawing, dated January 1955, shows an incomplete design as roof line and window abutment is quite pronounced. (Courtesy Citroën)

Just weeks before the DS's introduction (the drawing is dated 9th August 1955) Bertoni finally found the solution to the roof line problem. By extending the cantrail to form a trompette in which he could house the rear indicators, emphasis was diverted from the rear pillar. (Courtesy Citroën)

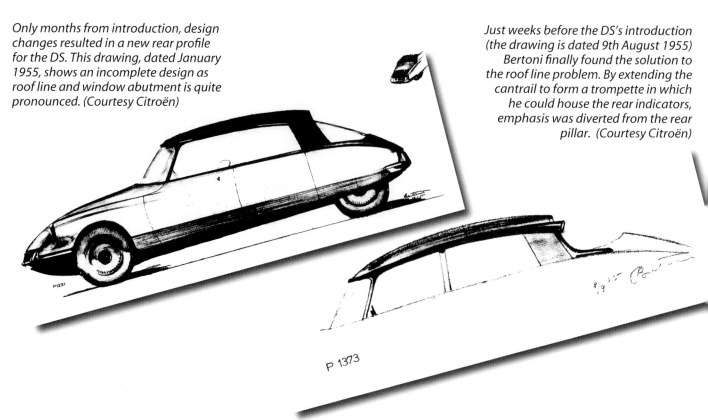

Bertoni was also concerned about the severity of the rear wings, so to resolve the issue he added embellishment to the rear reflectors which were originally rectangular in shape. The idea was to make the wings appear longer than they actually were, though ultimately the design was changed once the car was in production. The illustration shows the wing treatment of an early DS with the side embellishment removed. Undoing the single bolt allows removal of the wing when changing a wheel. (Author's collection)

230,000 examples were produced over a period of six years.

It would appear, then, that Bertoni's restyling of the VGD was undertaken as a calculated way of updating the project to take account of his latest thinking, something that was vitally important if the car was to remain in production long enough to recover the obviously enormous development costs. With the tooling process well under way Bertoni was limited to making only the most minor changes: there was no provision to alter the car's platform or body engineering although he did radically revise the roofline to give a severe roof and rear screen abutment. This severity of abutment is seldom noticed, thanks to the clever fitment of the direction indicators to form a continuation of the cantrail, a characteristic of these cars which resembles an elongated ice cream cornet. Anyone who has followed a DS will appreciate the positioning of the rear indicators which, being at eye level and separate from other lights on the car, are clearly visible in all traffic conditions.

Oddly, Citroën's lead in adopting high-mounted rear indicators was long ignored by other manufacturers, and it is only recently that they have become a feature on some modern vehicles. Bertoni's restyling also emphasised the profile of the rear wings, and by subtle embellishment to the reflectors he was able to make them appear longer than they actually were. The tail treatment of the DS is unique; the sharply raked boot lid giving access to a luggage compartment far more commodious than it would seem.

The speed with which Bertoni restyled the VGD is demonstrated by the fact that his revised drawings are dated January 1955, only nine months before the DS made its debut. This gave little time in which to finalise the tooling process and does credit to Citroën's designers and production engineers who were required to make many last minute adjustments.

SPACE AGE TECHNOLOGY

The VGD concept went far beyond Bertoni's controversial and futuristic styling. André Lefebvre's objective of the car succeeding the *Traction Avant* made full use of the latest engineering materials technology to the extent that everything before it would be immediately obsolete. Instead of continuing to use the by now universally adopted monocoque bodyshell, the VGD would consist of a punt-like platform, to which was welded a skeleton framework taking the form of a box-like structure known as the caisson. As with the 2CV, the car's front wheels were attached to leading arms, in-board brakes helping to reduce unsprung weight; the rear wheels were attached to trailing arms, the arrangement as a whole allowing much vertical wheel movement.

Because of the car's unique hydraulic suspension it was possible to choose an equally exceptional jacking method: using suspension technology, one side of the car could be effortlessly lifted to allow wheel changing. Removing a rear wing in order to change a wheel is not as difficult or bizarre as it may at first seem. Close

inspection reveals a single bolt head on the trailing edge of each wing; by undoing this with the appropriate spanner (or wheel nut brace on later cars) the entire wing panel can be easily detached. Wheel changing on a DS provides considerable entertainment for passers by!

The single-stud, centre-fixing, quick-release steel disc wheels fitted to early models are another unique feature. Manufactured by Michelin, the wheels incorporated a hexagonal socket so that, when mated to the hub and tightened with a special tool, the two locked together, a split boss on the hub assembly expanding as the screw fitting engaged with a conical plug. The DS was designed to use the newly introduced X radial tyre developed by senior Michelin engineer, Marius Mignol, during the war years. By changing the tyre's structure its lifespan was significantly increased and it gave greatly enhanced performance compared to cross-ply tyres. Introduction of the X gave Michelin a substantial lead over its rivals, and it was more than a decade before many car manufacturers were specifying radial tyres for their vehicles.

The caisson was designed to have great strength and rigidity, and be able to carry the vehicle's stresses. It also acted as a means of attaching the car's body panels, none of which, including the roof, was load-bearing. Hence, it was possible to form the roof from self-coloured fibreglass, and the bonnet from aluminium, this being the largest aluminium pressing used in any motorcar. (The boot lid

The DS was designed with a punt-like platform with front and rear sub-assemblies, onto which a skeleton framework was attached. The caisson supports the car's body panels and roof, none of which are load-bearing. This delightful publicity item succinctly illustrates the DS's construction and was published around the time the ID19 was introduced. If only everything was as simple … (Brian Chandler collection)

too until May 1957, after which steel was specified.) The fitting of fibreglass roofs throughout DS production wasn't universal; according to market and model requirement, such as cars built in the United Kingdom, aluminium was specified. Aluminium was adopted for those cars assembled outside France using the CKD process because

fibreglass panels were susceptible to transit damage. Aluminium also replaced fibreglass on French-built cars having black roofs to allow the alloy to be spray-painted.

The ample glass area - 25 per cent greater than that of the *Traction Avant* - is a noticeable feature of the VGD's styling, a contributing factor being

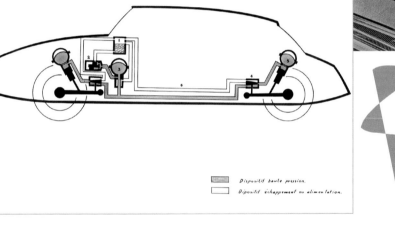

Dispositif haute pression.

Dispositif échappement ou alimentation.

Bertoni's use of curved screens, slim pillars, and frameless door windows. Not only did the slimness of the pillars aid visibility, but it also gave a sense of spaciousness within the car, and the frameless windows complemented the vehicle's overall radical design. With doors closed and window glasses raised, the pressure of the glass against the rubber seals effectively eliminated draughts and moisture.

The one feature of the car certain to evoke controversy is its use of hydropneumatics. Though the origins of the system have already been discussed, its apparent complexity has always provided those who doubt its reliability and effectiveness some fuel for argument. Essentially, Citroën's system uses a high pressure pump, belt-driven from the camshaft via the water pump pulley, to pressurise a gas-filled (in this instance nitrogen) accumulator. The fluid, fed from a reservoir in the engine compartment, assists in providing a pressure of 2490psi before being returned to its source. In the event of pressure falling below 2090psi, the pump operates to circulate the fluid until normal pressure is regained. Anyone used to riding in a DS, or any other hydropneumatic Citroën, will be familiar with the faint cacophony - a series of sighs and grunts - emanating from the hydraulic system.

As a means of self-levelling suspension, Citroën's arrangement reconciles the demands of comfort and sureness of roadholding: the car automatically remains perfectly level, maintaining constant ground clearance, whatever the number of passengers or amount of luggage carried. By keeping the body at a consistent level under varying static loads, minimum movement of the body and displacement of the centre of gravity is ensured. The all-round independent suspension is unique; instead of springs, hydropneumatic spheres absorb all shocks transmitted by the wheels, each linked to a piston working in a cylinder attached to the caisson. The vertical movements of the wheels are transmitted to a piston which, through the medium of hydraulic fluid in the cylinder, acts on the diaphragm in the sphere which contains compressed gas above the diaphragm. A damper valve between the cylinder and the sphere acts as a shock absorber, whilst valves, operated by the front and rear anti-roll bars, control the flow of hydraulic fluid to and from the cylinder, thus maintaining a constant height under varying static loads.

For anyone unsure of the system's reliability, look no further than the self-levelling arrangement which complements the coil springs and

TRIAL AND ERROR

The first clue to Citroën's radical proposals for the *Traction Avant's* successor emerged in May 1954, the *Traction Avant's* 20th anniversary. For what was obviously a production test bed for the forthcoming DS, the top-of-the-range six-cylinder Citroën was fitted with self-levelling rear suspension. A companion model to the 15 Six D, the 15 Six H - H referring to Hydropneumatique - was built in one model style, a five-seater saloon. The 15 Six D was built as a saloon and eight-seat familiale for the 1954 model year, the latter derivative was discontinued for 1955.

An initial glance at the 15 Six H revealed little about the car's revolutionary suspension, that is unless the vehicle had been standing idle for some time and the rear of the car

wishbone suspension of the Rolls-Royce Silver Shadow and Bentley T Series cars introduced in 1965. These - and subsequent models - used Citroën technology for the simple reason that manufacturers were unable to devise anything more efficient. The late John Hollings, chief engineer at Rolls-Royce Motor Cars, once told the author that efforts had been made to engineer a self-levelling system in-house. Rolls-Royce engineers were unable to match the quality and tolerances achieved by Citroën, which ultimately supplied the components to the firm's Crewe factory. Needless to say, the precision with which Citroën engineered its hydropneumatic system to give clearances of between 1 and 3 microns called for development skills quite unique within the motor industry at the time. When Citroën opened its factory at Asnières on the outskirts of Paris in 1954 to manufacture hydraulic system components, it represented the ultimate in micro-engineering. The operation was conducted with such expertise that it was possible to achieve previously inconceivable standards of engineering; for example, tolerances of 0.001mm, one fiftieth the thickness of a cigarette paper.

A car so futuristic as the DS used plastic where possible. Not only was a plastic engine cooling fan used for the first time, but interior fittings - particularly the moulded facia - predicted an age when, for British and European cars, polished wood veneers on all but the most specialist and prestigious cars would be consigned to history. An exponent of modern fabrics and bright colours, the DS was about to start a car culture as radical as its styling and technology.

When Citroën's six-cylinder Traction Avant *was fitted with self-levelling rear suspension (the 15 Six H) it was in effect a test bed for the forthcoming DS. A rare right-hand drive, Slough-built example belonging to Ray Andrews is shown here. (Author's collection)*

Under the bonnet of a six-cylinder Traction Avant fitted with rear self-levelling suspension. On this 15 Six H belonging to Steve Southgate can be seen the hydraulic fluid reservoir, the pipe from the top of the container connecting with the high pressure pump immediately aft of the radiator. (Author's collection)

had sunk on its haunches in nose-up attitude. This, then, was seemingly the pinnacle of achievement for Citroën's development team led by André Lefebvre and Paul Magès, except that something even more innovative was yet to be revealed ...

Testing of prototype VGDs had been carried out in total secrecy at Citroën's La Ferté-Vidame test track near Dreux in Normandy, fifty miles from Paris. Here, in fortress-like surroundings of twelve feet high exterior walls, the cars were tested to extreme, and always under the gaze of security guards mounted around the estate in watch towers, constantly on guard against inquisitive journalists and intruders. At the sign of any incursion, including aerial disturbance, sirens would sound and, on hearing the alarm, test personnel would drive their cars off the track and under the cover of buildings or trees. The exercise was not kept as quiet as Citroën officials might have hoped, and rumours began to circulate about the testing of fabulous cars about to be introduced.

It could well have been an April Fool's prank when, on 1st April 1952, the French motoring magazine, *l'auto-*

journal, carried the headline 'Nous avons filmé le prototype Citroën'. Even had it been a hoax the pictures which were reproduced show a vehicle sufficiently similar to prototype machines being tested at Dreux to be utterly convincing. There's little doubt these were genuine photographs, and the matter is all the more interesting because the pictures were taken by an opportunist photographer who happened to be near André Lefebvre's holiday retreat in the south of France.

With news leaked about the new Citroën, speculation about the impending car was rife in French newspapers. There was nothing for it but for Citroën to get on with perfecting the design as quickly as possible, and at least announcement of the Six H gave the company some time in which to finalise details and ready tooling for production. Citroën had a strict policy prohibiting personnel from disclosing information about the VGD project, but this did not prevent company workers from being coerced to reveal secrets by tempting sums of money. When in 1953 more leaked information was published in *l'auto journal* Citroën's plans were accurately exposed.

The 15 Six H meanwhile delighted motorists with its handling and performance coupled with seldom experienced ride quality. It was fascinating, after the car had been at rest, to see it lift at the rear to maintain a constant height despite load and number of passengers. Under the bonnet an indication of the car's hydropneumatics was a large cylindrical reservoir containing hydraulic fluid.

The comfort and ride quality of the Six H was a revelation, especially in France where roads remained in notoriously poor condition. The Six H was also assembled at Slough, and the British motoring press was eloquent in its praise. With road surfaces infinitely better than those in France, the car's qualities were not initially as obvious. Putting a Six H shod with Michelin X tyres through its paces, sweeping through quite severe bends at between 60 and 70mph, certainly impressed the correspondent writing in *The Motor* who declared it an encounter that had to be experienced to be believed.

The introduction of the Six-H confirmed that Citroën's new car was going to be something very different. Despite the *Traction Avant's* popularity, and the fact that it remained technically advanced compared to many cars, by 1955 styling standards it looked dated. In March 1955 in a review of the *Traction Avant* (701,000 examples of which were built), *The Motor* referred to the Six H as a superb motorcar with handling characteristics to match, "... but which is, in certain respects, lacking in modern amenities".

CHAPTER THREE

VOICI LA BOMBE CITROËN

If contemporary reports which emanated from France and elsewhere are to be believed, the DS's arrival in October 1955 was a surprise and the motor industry's best kept secret. This was not entirely true, though, as rumours about the new Citroën had been circulating since 1949, although the exact date of its launch remained a mystery. Nearly all the media's predictions about design and engineering concepts were speculative, except for those published by *l'auto journal* which were remarkably close to the truth.

Exposure of Citroën's futuristic design, courtesy of *l'auto journal*, was sufficient to send the rumour mill into freefall, and on both sides of 'La Manche' there was much anticipation of what would emerge from the Quai de Javel. For weeks, if not months, in advance of the Paris *Salon*, expectation grew that Citroën would unveil the *Traction Avant's* long-awaited successor, snippets of tantalising information serving to tease and generate further rumours and counter-rumours. At least one person claimed to have seen the DS on test ahead of its launch on the outskirts of Paris, and said it was

Citroën's successor for the Traction Avant *could not have been anything but a sensation, and the arrival of the DS in the autumn of 1955 lived up to expectation. Look at Renault's stand in the background where the Frégate is displayed: the product from Billancourt received scant attention compared to Javel's masterpiece. (Courtesy Citroën)*

'a dream car' but was reluctant to provide further detail. Whether the sighting was anything other than a flight of fancy or a deliberate attempt to excite controversy will remain a mystery since all pre-production cars - and there were around thirty of them - were assembled in complete secrecy and taken to La Ferté-Vidame for exhaustive testing. In addition to providing Citroën engineers with valuable information about necessary refinements before the car went into production, the prototype vehicles served as demonstrators throughout the Paris *Salon*, and thereafter as training vehicles for Citroën dealers and company personnel.

The pre-production cars were hardly representative of the definitive DS. Reports indicate that vehicles had

ill-fittings doors and panels, their finish lacked finesse, and they were noisy and prone to excessive vibration.

Happily, the cars destined to announce the Goddess at Paris, London and Geneva had no such shortcomings. They were carefully hand-built at the *Bureau d'Etudes* and not at Javel where, even in the wake of the Motor Show, the DS was a rare sight. Contrary to information that Citroën was feeding to the media, the car did not occupy production lines in great numbers; a mere seven cars were completed in October 1955, all within a sectionalised area of the factory known as the *bocale* where only a handful of selected employees - fewer than 100 out of a total of some 25,000 - were allowed access. By the end of the year no more than sixty-nine cars had left the factory.

Despite Citroën announcing the DS in the autumn of 1955, production of the car did not get under way until January 1956, and then only in moderate numbers, with 229 having left the factory by the end of the month. As the year progressed DS production got into its stride and by the year end a more encouraging figure of 9868 cars had been produced.

Serious problems existed with perfecting the car, and the situation was worse than when the *Traction Avant* was launched, a car considered as revolutionary as its successor. Never mind the frantic scenes of rectifying the DS's many problems that extensive testing revealed, the advent of the 42nd *Salon de L'Automobile* announced a new era in motor vehicle design.

When the *Salon* opened to the public on Thursday 6th October, the DS had already made its media debut the previous evening. The following morning newspapers ecstatically reported the car's arrival as the sensation of the year. Excited to near hysteria, visitors flocked to the Grand Palais in their thousands to see Citroën's offering.

'Voici La Bombe Citroën' was *l'auto journal's* headline which, in a nutshell, described how the car's dramatic debut stunned the nation. The huge amount of interest in the car throughout France can be understood, if only because the 'big five' of France - Citroën, Panhard, Renault, Simca, and Peugeot - collectively accounted for 99.97 per cent of all cars sold to French motorists.

The scene outside the Grand Palais has to be imagined: gendarmes fought to control the crowds, everyone jostling to be first into the exhibition to see the new Citroën for themselves. Within five minutes of the *Salon's* doors opening Citroën's stand was completely engulfed by spectators, the remainder of the hall virtually deserted. Even Citroën's salesmen were taken by surprise; it was several minutes before they gathered their wits enough to accept the handfuls of francs being thrust at them as deposits! Citroën enthusiast and president of the Citroën Car Club, Joe Judt who, over a long time has owned many cars bearing the Double Chevron in addition to Panhards, and now custodian of that most rare breed, an Henri Chapron *Décapotable*, recalls the first public

day at the Grand Palais: "The scene in the hall was frenetic and it was almost impossible to get close to the one DS on show. The name *Déesse* was on everyone's lips; most of the other manufacturers' stands were almost bare of spectators, and as a Citroën devotee I was too excited to think logically".

New cars, even by 1955 standards, and including the most prestigious and expensive, were often specified in mainly sombre colours, black seeming almost obligatory. Pastel shades at last became available, the DS exhibited at the Grand Palais boldly displaying its champagne body colour which contrasted wonderfully with an aubergine roof. The car's light coloured interior was a revelation, too, complementing the futuristic styling and emphasising the deeply cushioned front seats, which could be reclined in an instant to form a bed. Unlike the majority of cars on show, the DS had acres of leg room for rear seat passengers, enabling them to languish in total comfort.

Citroën's rivals looked on helplessly as crowds surged towards the DS. An element of mass hysteria was evident that first day of the *Salon*, which continued to a lesser extent throughout the show's ten day duration. Before the first day's trading had ended around one thousand DS orders were taken, rising to 80,000 by the end of the event. It seemed not to matter that buyers weren't given delivery dates; neither, for that matter, were there any cars to sell!

Despite the DS's radical design,

This monochrome photograph does little justice to the DS when it was shown at the 1955 Paris Motor Show. Most new cars wore sombre colours, but not the Goddess; she was painted Champagne with an Aubergine roof - very avant-garde! (Courtesy Citroën)

Ecstatic crowds greeted the President of France, René Coty, when he was introduced to the Goddess at the Paris Salon. With the President is Pierre Bercot, who nurtured the DS design process, having been delegated by Robert Puiseux to take over the car's development programme from Pierre Boulanger, who died at the wheel of an experimental Traction Avant in 1950. (Courtesy Citroën)

and the fact that, initially, none was available to sell, there remained a healthy market for the *Traction Avant* whose handling characteristics were still more advanced than some newly introduced designs. The furore the DS created at the *Salon* did not alleviate the scepticism of some, who believed the DS was too complicated with unproven technology. These customers generally opted for the *Traction*, which remained in production in France until 1957.

The debate that went on behind closed doors at Citroën's rivals in the wake of the DS's unveiling can only be guessed at. In 1949 Renault had abandoned development of a stylish and streamlined rear-engined 2-litre car. Ultimately the Frégate, Billancourt's answer to the *Traction Avant*, was a breath of fresh air when introduced in 1950, it's modern styling - even with an American influence - standing out in a motor industry recovering from war. In the shadow of the DS, however, the Frégate appeared dated, with nothing to directly replace it until Renault's hatchback 16 arrived in the mid-sixties.

At Sochaux, Peugeot, having pinned its post war hopes on the solidly reliable 203 in 1948 - again, with American influenced styling - may well have expected that the 203's successor, the tough and virtually indestructible 403 with Pininfarina flair, would be the star of the '55 *Salon* until upstaged by Citroën. Post war Panhards were utterly unconventional, the Dyna giving way to the PL17 which, in Tigre disguise, was capable of outpacing some of the most athletic machines. Panhard

was acquired by Citroën in 1965, but after just two years this most famous of marques had become obsolete. As for Simca, prewar the company had produced Fiats under licence, but the Vedette failed to attract customers in the anticipated numbers, and the marque mainly concentrated on medium size saloons, the Aronde being its best seller.

Elsewhere in Paris the sensational arrival of *la bombe Citroën* at Citroën's showroom in the Champs Elysées resulted in a queue of people four deep and half a mile long. Citroën dealers and journalists were properly acquainted with the Goddess over *déjeuner* at Le Restaurant Ledoyen, nearby in the Champs Elysées, a sumptuous banquet for 400 guests courtesy of Javel's directors. Following *la langouste, le caneton, les fromages* and *le glacé Sibérian*, all nicely complemented by Pommard 1949 and Laurens Brut, the party was taken by bus to the outskirts of the city where twenty DS19s awaited. The sight of the cars, each reclining but ready to spring to life in an instant, was amazing. Citroën's test drivers were instructed by company management to demonstrate to their passengers the DS's proficiency in travelling over surfaces apparently designed to test a car's suspension to its limit. One motoring journalist wrote of the occasion: "In spite of speed and what might be called reckless driving, there was that feeling of security coupled with comfort. That one ride was worth the visit to Paris, it was something I never want to forget and something I will never forget."

Not all visitors to the *Salon* received the VIP treatment, Joe Judt remarking that he would have willingly given his right arm to experience a ride in one of the twenty DSs available to special guests. Neither, despite the throngs of spectators converging on the Citroën display, were all visitors totally impressed by the DS. Among these was the late Bill Allen, a brilliant designer and stylist who began work in 1928 at the age of 16 with coachbuilder Arthur Mulliner Ltd of Northampton, and who subsequently worked for Rover and Rolls-Royce. Bill remained at Rolls-Royce until he retired, and in his capacity as assistant to the chief stylist his input with all of the firm's cars, including Derby and Crewe Bentleys, was enormous. He was deeply involved in the design of models such as the Silver Cloud and S-series Bentley, the Silver Shadow (the company's first monocoque design), Corniche, and a succession of Phantoms.

Bill was present at the unveiling of the DS and, like everyone else, was astonished at what he saw. Travelling with the author many years later, a DS was spotted, prompting Bill to recount his recollections of seeing the DS for the first time. He was adamant that the car was the ugliest he had ever seen, and he certainly did not share the popular view that it was of exceptional design. Even the fact that Rolls-Royce used Citroën technology in the Silver Shadow's self-levelling system did not change his opinion. His dislike of the DS extended from the shape of the car's drooping bonnet, the absence of a conventional air intake, the tail and

The build process of the DS at Javel. Here, operatives are welding the skeleton bodyshell, the rear screen being nearest the camera. (Courtesy Citroën)

Pictured at Javel, the skeleton of the DS may appear somewhat fragile, though it does, in fact, possess great strength. Unlike the monocoque adopted by many manufacturers, the framework or base unit as seen here allowed body panels to be mainly bolted in place. (Courtesy Citroën)

feature was blissfully unaware of what lay in store when the *Salon's* doors opened the following morning, for the feature questioned whether the car's innovations would be acceptable to the buying public. There was caution, too, about the car's advanced technology: "It is difficult to assess at the moment what sort of reception the car will receive. It moves into a higher price bracket than previous Citroën models by approximately £150. It is bristling with interesting features, but they are, of necessity, rather complex, and the maze of hydraulic pipes with their circuits, dependent upon one belt-driven hydraulic pump, may result in some apprehension on the part of would-be purchasers, and this might affect its commercial success."

The name Flaminio Bertoni obviously meant little to *The Autocar's* journalist, for the design of the DS was wrongly attributed to the Italian firm of Bertone. Furthermore, the car's styling was likened to that of the Bristol sports car. As *The Autocar* was cautious in its reportage, its newsstand contemporary, *The Motor*, was much more optimistic in its review of the Goddess. "Two-litre French car at under £1,000 with self-adjusting pneumatic suspension and hydraulic operation of steering, brakes, clutch and gearbox" was surely enough to get readers out of their armchairs and along to their nearest Citroën dealership. In promising DS customers that they would have the "... unprecedented

rear wing arrangement, and last but not least, the car's construction and interior layout. Forty years after first seeing the DS, in which time styling developments had appreciably changed, Bill did not alter his opinion.

'Citroën DS19 Startles Paris' was the initial verdict of *The Autocar* on the occasion of the *Salon* preview, the evening before the *Salon's* public opening. Obviously, the writer of the

In skeleton form the DS arrives at a point on the assembly line where the engine and gearbox are fitted. (Courtesy Citroën)

chance of travelling well, fast and in safety", the same journal said of the car's introduction in Paris that it had "... enough effect to allow the rest of the show to fall flat on its face."

Road & Track was far and away the most objective about the car, coming to the conclusion that it was almost too fascinating. Impressed by the fact that its gadgetry was an integral part of the design, and therefore an aid to reducing driver effort to an absolute minimum rather than merely extra cost contrivances, it said that the DS successfully departed from convention to give safe and comfortable transportation.

For American motorists used to cars with ultra-soft suspension and effortless automatic transmission suited to long-distance cruising, the DS was a delight. Some motorists might have wondered why Citroën did not develop a fully automatic gearbox, but at least gear changing demanded nothing more than easing one's foot off the accelerator and finger-light movement on the steering column-mounted switch. The term 'switch' is used in preference to 'lever' since the latter suggests that an element of effort is required. In reality the gear selector, positioned on the top of the steering column, needed only the slightest touch. Not even the softest and most wallowing springing of American machines could match the efficiency of Citroën's hydropneumatic system, which absorbed every shock whilst maintaining a degree of stability never before achieved.

America developed a love affair

with the Goddess from the moment she made her debut. The car's shape, technological wizardry and charisma was in such complete contrast to the chrome and fins American motorists had been used to that her success was immediately assured.

John C. Fitch, writing in Esquire magazine, declared the car to be a living, breathing piece of machinery that would capture the imagination of even the most conservative motorist: "Here is a no-spoke steering-wheeled automotive offbeat which powers everything, including the jack, with a seven-cylinder oil pump. She is sleek and beautiful in front, but short, blunt and baffling at the rear. At rest she squats like a tired dachshund, but when the engine is started she grandly rises to the job and to a working height automatically suited to the load. She will obligingly pick up her feet to change shoes, sparing you the trouble of fighting a jack, or pick up her skirts (and her ground clearance) and carry you over a small cliff. She is road-clinging, front-wheel drive, and, at first glance, brakeless. The power brake pedal is instead a small button looking much like a headlamp dimmer switch, and the spare wheel is carried in front of the radiator. In spite of this the DS19 is an exceptionally safe, comfortable

car scheduled for mass production by a healthy and venerable French firm; she promises eventually to deserve her admiring nickname, The Goddess, but until her extravagant intricacies are fully mastered she will be somewhat inconstant. The maintenance of a fancy woman was ever so. The Citroën undoubtedly has the most advanced engineering features of any production car in the world today, yet it remains a paradox".

After the glitter and passion that was Paris it was time for the Goddess to make her debut at London's Earls Court. British motorists, having witnessed the adoration bestowed upon her by Parisians, were in no doubt about the Goddess's celebrity status. Earls Court, too, was besieged by motorists and would-be car owners, each wanting to see the latest on offer from a motor industry emerging from post war austerity, and that meant having a long look at the latest Citroën.

It was Laurence Pomeroy's belief that the 1955 Paris and London Motor Shows were the most significant since introduction of front-wheel brakes on motorcars. In his capacity as technical editor of The Motor, Pomeroy viewed developments at the Grand Palais and Earls Court as the writing on the wall,

continued page 54

Now looking more like a car, the part-built DS has the windscreen in place along with the running gear. The car's centre fixing wheels are shown to good effect here; note how skinny the Michelin X tyres look. Also evident is the hydraulic system reservoir and the exhaust system, the silencer just forward of the gearbox and placed across the car. Note the slave wheels fitted to the rear of the leading car, and other cars in this picture. (Courtesy Citroën)

The fibreglass roof is going on; the next stage is to fit the doors and bonnet. (Courtesy Citroën)

DSs undergoing the final stages of construction, with doors and bonnets in place. On the left of the picture Traction Avants can be seen in a late phase of assembly. Note the forward positioning of the spare wheel on the DS, in the centre of which can be seen the stand which supports the car during wheel changing. (Courtesy Citroën)

Above: Finished cars are coming off
the production line at Javel. Behind
the partition a Traction Avant is seen
preparing to leave the assembly line.
(Courtesy Citroën)

Left: The delivery hall at Javel where
DSs, Tractions, and H Vans are awaiting
despatch. (Courtesy Citroën)

Right: When the DS arrived at Citroën
dealerships it generated huge interest.
This is Citroën's prestigious showroom
on the Champs-Élysées in the autumn
of 1957 when HM The Queen visited
Paris, hence the presence of the
Union flag, together with drapes
representing the Tricolor. The car
centre right is an ID19 - note the
wheels minus full-size hub caps and
the painted headlamp bezels. The
2CV and Tractions make interesting
comparisons to the DS.
(Courtesy Citroën)

such were the technological advances demonstrated by various motor manufacturers. Styling characteristics determined that the full-width body, once clumsy-looking, was relieved by downward sloping bonnets and boots; and a trend was emerging whereby the top half of the body was composed almost entirely of glass; materials other than steel, for example fibreglass, were used for bodywork, and greater attention was paid to performance and a variety of accessories, especially radios. The DS's huge technological leap prompted Laurence Pomeroy to conclude that: "Automobile design can never be quite the same".

At the opening ceremony of the Earls Court London Motor Show a specially constructed right-hand drive DS was the centre of attention, brought to England from France by Ken Smith who can justifiably claim to be the first person to drive a DS on British soil. Ken was guardian to this exquisite and expensive piece of machinery, his experience with the Goddess beginning with test driving prototype cars at Ferté-Vidame. Ken was sent to the *Bureau d'Etudes* by Louis Garbe, charismatic managing director of Citroën Cars Ltd whose fondness for Britain was equal to that for his native France.

Ken Smith brought the first right-hand drive DS to Britain in time for a reception and presentation at Citroën's Slough factory on the evening of Friday 7th October to coincide with the opening of the Paris Motor Show. To reach his destination, Ken left Paris at dawn the previous day, the intention being that he would arrive at Slough that evening, allowing twenty-four hours in which to have the car made ready for the event. The journey, which meant conveying two cars in a covered lorry for the sake of secrecy, did not go as planned. The intention was to travel to Dunkerque, disembark the cars at the port and load them aboard a ferry and sail to Dover, where they would be loaded onto a waiting lorry for the journey to Slough. Instructions from the *Bureau d'Etudes* were implicit inasmuch that the cars were not to be driven on the road, under any circumstances, but this order was overturned by Citroën Cars' managing director in the interest of getting the vehicles to Slough in time for their appointment with the media.

On arrival at Dunkerque conditions in the Channel were such that ships were prevented from leaving port until gales had abated and the sea had become calmer. Ken's schedule by then had been delayed by twelve hours, which meant that, had he waited for the cars to be transported by lorry to Slough, they would not have arrived in time. The alternative was for him to drive one of the cars to the factory, arriving there at precisely five o'clock to be greeted by journalists and local dignitaries, as well as the entire company workforce, intent on seeing the DS.

So Ken Smith was the first person to experience a long-distance drive in a DS on a public highway, from the channel coast to Slough. Ken's reception at Slough will remain in his memory forever: everyone was flabbergasted at seeing the car, as its design had been kept secret from even Citroën employees. The two DSs remained carefully concealed at Slough until the opening of the London Motor show on 19th October, where company personnel had the opportunity to become acquainted with the cars and learn about their technology.

For Ken Smith the cars' arrival was the end result of a year's work in Paris assisting in the development of right-hand drive examples destined for assembly at Slough. In order to construct the DS in Britain the Slough works would have to be drastically reorganised with new manufacturing facilities, a task that would fully occupy Ken's time. An account of the Slough operation is to be found elsewhere in this book, but it's relevant to establish here that, like the British and Commonwealth market *Traction Avant*, the Slough DS would be uniquely different to its French-built sibling.

While one of the two cars brought from Paris was prepared for Earls Court, the other was destined to be a familiarisation vehicle for UK Citroën dealers. Among the first to examine the car was John Poxon of Worthing Motors, the first garage in Britain to be appointed a Citroën agency. Fifty years on John's impression of the DS is historic and revealing, for it really is the first in-depth report of the car.

"Having had occasion to visit the Citroën factory at Slough I was indeed most fortunate to be able to examine very closely one of the new 2-litre DS19s in a partly dismantled state, and I must say how impressed I was with the accessibility of all components. For

any major repair the front wings can be removed in a matter of minutes, rather like the 2CV. Once these are removed, the majority of the front end is laid bare, and is therefore easier to work on than is the case with most cars. It would appear that, for ordinary decarbonising operations, one could readily take off the wings before work commenced, thereby not only facilitating the actual job, but also safeguarding the paintwork.

"After spending some time examining the working parts of the car, M Garbe [managing director of Citroën Cars Ltd] very kindly offered to take me out for a run, which I was delighted to accept and, after receiving a certain amount of instruction, I drove the car myself. I must say that before this, I had always felt that the power steering might take a little getting

used to, especially if one likes, as I do, to feel the steering. However, my fears were rapidly dispelled, and although there is no feeling at all on the steering, it is uncannily accurate - with not the slightest trace either of over - or under - steer that one immediately feels quite at home. It is not at all comparable with the ordinary form of light steering and is absolutely in a class by itself - it has to be tried to be believed. Corners can be taken at any speed with complete confidence after but a few minutes' driving.

"The next point about which I was a little dubious was the gear shift, but this again is indeed incredibly simple to operate. One merely selects first gear and accelerates hard for a fast get-away, or gently in order to move forward slowly. To change to second gear it is only necessary to ease the

foot slightly on the accelerator pedal, engage second gear and immediately accelerate. This is a perfectly natural movement and all the other gears operate in the same way, there being no need to take either hand from the steering wheel in the normal manner, two fingers fall naturally to the lever for all gear selections and it seems, indeed, difficult to make any mistake. I have driven cars with fully automatic transmission and, frankly, do not like them as I find it more than somewhat disconcerting to feel that the gear is changed without my direct control. The DS19 has all the advantage of the fully automatic box, but with the further advantage that the moment chosen for the change is left to the discretion of the driver, which personally I think is most important.

"The braking system, which I also

felt might prove a little difficult to start with is, again, quite natural and one is not really conscious of the fact that the usual pedal is missing, its place being taken by a small rubber button on the floor. The touch on this button is, perhaps, rather delicate, but at the same time positive and very progressive.

"Over the course we had some fast stretches and on one of these an indicated speed of 73mph in third gear was attained. I must say that the ratios chosen throughout the whole of the gearbox seem ideal. The acceleration in third gear between 40mph and 70mph is perfect for overtaking in heavy traffic conditions. There is complete absence of any gear whine in this speed range and it is possible to remain in third for long periods. Fourth gear is a very high gear and gives the impression of a manually operated overdrive. What speed the car will achieve in top I did not have the opportunity to discover, but by the general feel I should image 90mph could be reached. In some of the twisty lanes we drove through the real usefulness of the power steering became apparent, and on one particular hairpin bend - which would have proved impossible for the Light Fifteen or Six Cylinder to negotiate in one turn - was taken at quite reasonable speed with no effort whatsoever.

"We next took the car over an unmade road, pitted with deep potholes and with a very loose gravel surface. The ride under these conditions was perfect and very few road shocks were felt in the car, the most noticeable thing being the noise of the tyres over the gravel and the rattling of stones

on the underside of the body. In an open area, with a similar bad surface, I tried the lock and also the steering for surface effects. There was absolutely no reaction even over the roughest road, either over the straight or on full lock, and one could safely let go of the wheel which would remain in position without the slightest tremor.

"For parking the power steering is invaluable; one can easily turn the wheel from lock to lock with the car stationary. Not that this is necessarily a good thing to do, but with our congested roads and the difficulty of finding a parking space, one often has to do this, and together with the car's enormous lock, parking should present no problems at all.

"The day was a cold one when I tried the car and so proved an excellent opportunity to test the heating installation; in only a few minutes it was necessary to reduce the heat intake. The other point that impressed me about the air-conditioning was the cold air vents at the front. As far as I could see the car is so adequately ventilated for hot or cold air there is virtually no need to open the windows at all."

Before the DS officially went into production in January 1956, behind-the-scenes work was hectic, monitoring the performance of 500 pre-production cars that were intended for selected customers. To be a selected customer meant being known to Citroën as a long-term loyal enthusiast who was prepared to report on the car's reliability and performance on a regular basis, and to accept that, as a new and highly innovative design, it might at

times experience no end of teething troubles. Members of the Michelin family were on the select customer list, as were dignitaries and diplomats who would be seen as good ambassadors for Citroën.

Selected customers knew full well that they were acting in an experimental capacity on behalf of Citroën, and that there would inevitably be problems with the cars, hopefully not too serious but nonetheless inconvenient and annoying. The trial and error strategy embarked upon by Citroën engineers was to keep the pilot batch of vehicles under close scrutiny and collect all necessary data, essential for the introduction of modifications as and when required.

By agreeing to become a pilot user selected customers were obliged to adhere to a number of conditions; namely to report malfunctions immediately, to allow Citroën engineers to regularly examine the cars, and to agree not to compromise the car's reputation in any way. Restrictions on use were explicit: cars should not be parked overnight in a public place for fear of the inquisitive taking too close a look at the vehicle; nor was the car's technology to be demonstrated to anyone. Cars were not to be taken to Citroën agents in the event of a technical problem or breakdown, but instead Citroën engineers were to be consulted direct via a dedicated department. Because of Citroën's determination to keep DS development a total secret there was an absence of product familiarisation for dealers, which meant that when the

Citroën produced some controversial publicity material for the DS during the 1950s, the two examples depicted here dating from late in that decade. Both evoke a feeling of surrealism, the adventurously pastel coloured cars appearing out of proportion to their surroundings. Spot the difference between the yellow and green cars: the green vehicle has painted headlamp rims while the wheels sport minimal caps protecting the centre fixing bolt, thus identifying it as an ID19. (Brian Chandler collection)

Citroën

car did go on sale there was little in the way of information to allow even the most minor problem to be remedied.

For customers who placed orders for the DS at the 1955 *Salon* there was an agonisingly long wait before cars were delivered. When they did arrive the cars suffered all sorts of technical problems, and dealers were ill-equipped to rectify them. The complex technology of the DS proved a nightmare for Citroën's agents, some of whom refused to handle problematic cars, preferring instead to dispatch them to the factory for repair or modification. A number of agents believed such a radical car would be the cause of financial ruin and terminated their dealerships with Citroën.

The situation at Citroën was grave, and seemingly insurmountable. Problems not evident on prototype vehicles suddenly manifested themselves on production vehicles, because production line operatives had developed practices not previously used on cars hand-built at the *Bureau d'Etudes*. These were mainly associated with the hydraulics; seals failed, there were fluid leakages, gear selection was often inoperable, and stories abounded of cars being stuck in gear and immobilized.

There was a real danger that Citroën's reputation was suffering irreparable damage. News of these problems spread quickly, and no doubt Citroën's rivals watched the unfortunate spectacle from afar, acquiring new customers as a result. In addressing the problems Citroën established a squad of engineers experienced in DS technology: whenever problems occurred with a customer's car they rushed to the scene by the most appropriate and quickest method - car, train or aeroplane - in the interest of quickly getting the vehicle back on the road. The squad, Citroën's *Super Contrôle*, was first established in the 1930s in the wake of the *Traction's* introduction to oversee that model's initial problems, and now spearheaded the campaign to perfect the DS.

Some of the problems associated with DS production procedures were the result of ignorance on the part of assembly personnel. Hydraulic system seals were pressed into position using screwdrivers, thus damaging them before vehicles had even left the factory. Indifferent fitting of clutch and steering components was also to blame; in time all procedures were examined and revised methods introduced.

Javel was besieged with DSs returned to the factory by dealers unable, or unwilling, to carry out necessary repairs. This situation led to the establishment of a rectification shop, manned largely by apprentices in order to minimise costs whilst providing essential training. Here, vehicles were repaired and returned to their owners in double-quick time.

There's no denying that early problems experienced with the DS affected sales; the second-hand market for DSs collapsed, and potential customers of new cars had to be enticed back to the marque by a series of sales campaigns designed to remind motorists what an innovative car the DS was.

Joe Judt, who had been in Paris for the launch of the DS, first sampled the car courtesy of Alistair Macdonald, then a salesman at London Citroën agent Normans of Westminster before he was appointed sales manager at Citroën's Slough headquarters. Joe recalls that: "The experience was mind-boggling, more so a culture shock! I felt my then *Traction* was a great car, but totally dated by this virtually outer space conveyance".

Asked whether he thought the car was too futuristic, Joe's reply was definite: "Good heavens, no! I simply had to have one and there and then placed my order, colour blue and cream. No-one told me that I would have to wait a year or more to finally secure delivery, the price shot up twice whilst I was waiting; nevertheless I had to have my DS. Driving through London's streets in the car was an eerie experience, it was like sitting in a glass house, continuously stared at, fingers pointed - 'Daddy, what's that funny looking car?' As for the constant activities of the DS suspension, many other drivers of lesser machines, as well as pedestrians, gaped open-mouthed in wonder and astonishment, necks craning to get a closer look. For myself, 1956, the car was delivered in September, is a year I shall never forget to my last day."

Quite a few dealers in the United Kingdom were upset by having to wait a year as no DSs were available. The first few produced at Slough went to New Zealand and Australia (as far away as possible from Slough's point of view), as a sort of testing ground: after all, it was

Citroën was keen to sell the DS to business users, hence the industrial backdrop. (Brian Chandler collection)

to sell but seemingly endless waiting lists, plus irate customers waiting in vain for their Goddess. *Traction* production in the UK had ceased, resulting in even more irate customers (quite a few loyal Citroën customers wanted to buy the obsolete model, assuming one could be had), and lost revenue for the dealers.

rather difficult to complain from that distance about the constant leakage of red hydraulic fluid which plagued the early cars! A number of dealers were forced to relinquish their dealership arrangements with the UK company or face financial ruin: there were no cars

Viewed from this angle the elegance of the Goddess can be fully appreciated - and naturally Citroën's publicity department ensured that chic fifties fashions helped set the scene. This publicity photograph exemplifies the upsweep of the bonnet to partially hide the windscreen wipers, the positioning of the interior mirror on the facia, and the tell-tale lights-on indicators on the wing tops. (Courtesy Citroën)

i q u e

UN CONFORT TOTAL

La notion de confort a été enrichie de tout ce qui peut favoriser les aises des passagers.

L'HABITABILITÉ

GÉNÉROSITÉ DES DIMENSIONS INTÉRIEURES : 5 places confortables. Grâce au large empattement de la voiture, l'espace pour les genoux entre la banquette arrière et le dossier avant est le plus grand de toutes les voitures françaises.

On peut ainsi dormir à l'arrière comme à l'avant les jambes allongées. Ajoutons que le plancher est absolument plat.

DES SIÈGES OÙ VOUS SEREZ À L'AISE : ces sièges-couchettes sont individuels et réglables. Seul le nylon, textile moderne, pouvait convenir aux sièges de la DS. Jersey rhovenyl ou nylon helanca, ces tissus ont été étudiés tant sur le plan de leurs coloris que sur celui de leur texture pour répondre à un cahier des charges très précis : élastiques, lavables, ils s'offrent dans une gamme très large de coloris.

POUR LES BAGAGES, UNE SOUTE PLUS QU'UN COFFRE : entièrement disponible, elle est si profonde qu'on peut y disposer des valises verticalement. Sa contenance est de 1/2 m3, ses parois planes et rectangulaires permettent un chargement complet avec des valises normales.

Above & right: Stylish publicity material was created for the American market, into which a degree of artistic licence has crept. Unusual that a rear three-quarter view is portrayed, which in this instance captures the essence of the marketing theme.
(Brian Chandler collection)

This publicity item graphically illustrates the vast interior space of the DS, along with the ample luggage capacity.
(Brian Chandler collection)

Citroën technology is forefront in this American market publicity illustration. By the time the DS made its appearance the majority of American cars sported exaggerated styling themes, including slab-sided coachwork, wide, flat bonnets and trunks, and massive fins. By comparison the DS appeared quite modest in size, hence the need to remind potential customers of the Citroën's fabulous ride and handling. Note the pod-type front direction indicators and the Citroën script on the bonnet. (Brian Chandler collection)

Citroën

CITROEN CARS CORPORATION
300 PARK AVENUE, NEW YORK, N. Y.
ELDORADO 5-2872

Hydropneumatique
DS 19 CITROËN

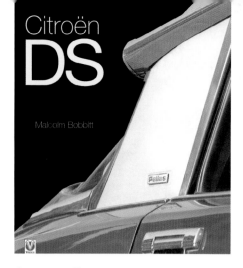

Citroën DS

Malcolm Bobbitt

CHAPTER FOUR

A BONNE IDÉE

The early life of the DS was beset with problems, which, in a car as innovative and technically advanced as the DS, is hardly surprising. Much of the trouble emanated from the vehicle's hydraulic system, and countless DS owners experienced the exasperation of leaking pipes, resulting in pools beneath the car which had sunk low on its haunches after being stationary for a time. These owners quickly realised that the car's red-coloured, castor-based hydraulic fluid - typically Lockheed HD19 or Castrol HF - was hardly user-friendly; spill some on the paintwork at your peril ...

The automatic adjustment of the ride height also came in for some criticism until Citroën engineers, responding to complaints from customers and dealers alike, added a manually-operated height adjustment lever in February 1956. Installed on the left-hand chassis sidemember adjacent to the pendant parking brake (remaining in this position on right-hand drive vehicles), the lever allowed for five suspension settings: low, normal, two intermediates, and high. For everyday driving the normal setting gave optimum comfort whilst the two intermediate positions were ideal for towing purposes as they gave a firmer ride.

Another complaint was that the DS could, at times, be unpredictable

During the 1930s Citroën adopted 'Floating Power' technology for its cars which was characterised by a swan in water. For the '50s a similar theme showed the DS floating on water to epitomise its smooth ride. This is a typical example of Citroën's publicity department's sometimes bizarre approach to marketing; how successful it is will be a matter of personal opinion. (Brian Chandler collection)

when manoeuvring at slow speed and low engine revs, a shortcoming that was remedied in March 1956 by modifying the carburettor idling device to provide a smooth take-up of the transmission. Then there was the problem of hydraulic fluid overheating, which Citroën's engineers resolved by introducing apertures in the top of the front wings, covered with aluminium grilles (later changed to stainless steel) which became known as *cendriers* but which looked more like cheese graters or drain covers. This modification - on DS models only by virtue of a more complex hydropneumatic set-up - was introduced between September 1959 and September 1962 to improve under-bonnet airflow. Ironically, the modification led to an over-abundance of cold or freezing air in winter and blanking plates were supplied to cover the grilles when conditions required.

Citroën would not acknowledge that the DS's introduction and programme of trouble-shooting had exerted a severe strain on company resources, but years later, when recalling the months following the car's debut, Pierre Bercot revealed just how serious a crisis had existed. Apart from the *Traction Avant*, production of which was scaled down in 1955 in order to prioritise the DS, and scheduled to end in 1957, the only other model in the Citroën catalogue was the utilitarian and corrugated-looking 2CV, sales of which were, fortunately, sufficiently buoyant to enable ongoing DS development. *Traction* production had fallen from 61,100 units in 1953 to 52,320 in 1954, no doubt due in part to the rumours that were circulating about the new car; 44,362 were built in 1955, 39,395 in 1956, and just 3682 in 1957. During the same period 2CV output trebled, from 34,800 to more than 107,251 examples; had it not done so, injecting much needed cash into Citroën's coffers, there's reason to believe that the company may not have survived this critical time.

Compared to the newly introduced DS, the *Traction Avant* had become so familiar throughout Europe that its technology - once considered particularly complex - held no concerns for even the smallest and most basically equipped rural garage. The French approach to engineering matters meant that problems - simple or otherwise - were quickly identified. Outside of France the car's front-wheel drive and requirement for special tools in order to perform specific tasks was largely understood. Unlike the DS with its complicated hydraulics, the *Traction* was considered straightforward, and could be driven for thousands of kilometres with only the most essential maintenance.

There was also the question of cost. The DS was more expensive than the model it replaced, which, for many prospective customers, was a disincentive; even the DS's luxurious interior was a matter of concern to those happier with a more utilitarian finish that was highly durable and less expensive. As for farmers, what did they want with luxuries such as carpets and jersey upholstery when rubber matting and cord fabrics were more resilient to their working environment?

Farmers might not have wanted luxury, but certain businesspeople did, and for them Citroën obliged by introducing the DS Prestige in October 1958. This was a truly luxurious vehicle with every conceivable accessory, including a central division with electric or manual glass lift according to preference, which made it a limousine in the true sense. Before WW2 the most affluent and demanding of French motorists could choose from marques such as Delage, Delahaye or Hotchkiss in which to travel, and even Renault and Panhard built 'official' cars. With the disappearance after the war of the grandes marques, Citroën's six-cylinder models were virtually the only choice for the most discerning clientele. Built to special order only, the Prestige remains among the rarest of DS saloons with around 180 examples delivered.

Each Prestige was finished to customer specification by coachbuilder, Henri Chapron, at Levallois on the north western outskirts of Paris. Equipment included separate front and rear sunroofs, a telephone - at the time quite novel and possibly the first time one was used in a motor vehicle, though reception was restricted to within 20 kilometres of the centre of Paris - and lighting in both compartments. Nearly everything was possible for those customers who insisted on total luxury, from provision of picnic tables in the rear compartment to a drinks cabinet and even a television. Front compartments were fitted with a leather upholstered bench seat

The DS's complex technology, together with its relatively high price compared to the Traction Avant, *prompted Citroën to introduce a simplified version of the car with less reliance on hydraulics. When the ID19 was unveiled at the 1956 Paris Motor Show it was greeted with enthusiasm by potential customers who would not otherwise have purchased the DS. Here, Pierre Bercot introduces the ID19 to Général de Gaulle at the 1958 Paris Salon. (Courtesy Citroën)*

that had adjustable cushions, and the rear compartment was furnished in grey cloth. Needless to say, the DS's 6-volt electrical system was hopelessly inadequate, so the Prestige was fitted with a 12-volt system which was eventually adopted across the entire model range.

SIMPLIFYING THE DS

Some loyal Citroën customers considered that the DS was unnecessarily complicated but still appreciated the car's advanced styling, superbly forgiving suspension, and generous interior accommodation. For them, power steering, hydraulic gear selection, and braking by way of a mushroom-shaped floor button were far from essential features (despite the physical exertion necessary to haul the steering wheel from lock-to-lock whilst parking).

The cost of the DS's technology and other attributes posed something of a problem for Citroën. Peugeot was selling the 403 Grande Luxe at 735,000 francs, some 87,500 francs more expensive than the *Traction Avant* 11BL; Renault's handsome 2-litre Frégate commanded 761,500 francs, whilst the luxury Amiral version cost another 125,500 francs. Even Simca's Vedette in its most luxurious form, the Versaille, was priced at 890,000 francs, some 175,000 francs cheaper than the DS. Faced with losing sales to rival

manufacturers, and given that there was obviously a need for it, Citroën was driven to devise a less complicated version of the DS, which would meet the demands - and wallets - of a significant number of customers.

In essence the move to produce a de-trimmed, de-tuned (66bhp) and mechanically simpler derivative of the existing DS, the price of which had risen to more than 1,065,000 francs by the spring of 1957, seemed relatively easy. What proved more difficult was achieving a substantial price reduction in order to more closely match the *Traction's* lead-in price of 647,500 francs. The DS was an expensive car to build and there was little scope for cost savings, which meant that when Citroën did its sums and arrived at a price tag of 860,000 francs for a model that was truly basic but nevertheless remarkably advanced, no-one objected too much. This figure could buy you the Normale, an ultra-utilitarian model which proved too spartan and underpowered even for those customers seeking total frugality. Using the Normale (more of which later) as a comparison, Citroën dealers had little difficulty persuading potential customers to pay an additional 65,000 francs for considerably more refinement in the shape of the ID19, which was priced at 925,000 francs. Customers who opted for the ID19 in preference to the very basic Normale had the satisfaction of knowing they

were saving 140,000 francs on the cost of the more luxurious and technically sperior DS19.

However, a less expensive derivative, selling in substantial numbers, would ultimately eat into Citroën's profits, the original calculations and projections having been based on the DS.

One year after Citroën launched the DS19, the ID19 made its debut at the Paris Motor Show. In choosing the ID (*Idée*) nomenclature Citroën cleverly retained the DS association so that what exhibition visitors saw was a car which appeared virtually identical to its Goddess sister car. It was only on closer examination that the differences between the two models became apparent: much of the DS's interior refinement was lost to a much more basic arrangement, the Luxe version being devoid of luxuries with reclining seats replaced by static versions, and plain door panels without armrests. Costs were pared to the extent that the roof was unlined and door furnishings were formed from cheaper materials than those used for the Goddess; carpeting was sacrificed in the interest of economy, replaced with simple rubber matting.

Externally the ID19 could be identified by wheel trims in the form of a small chrome cap concealing the locking nut, and also by its brown plastic rear indicator trompettes. There were plain painted aluminium rear pillars, and the rear wings were fitted with round reflectors. Instead of the DS's uniquely aesthetically-pleasing facia and instrumentation, that of the

ID was purely conventional; for Citroën at any rate. The steering wheel, still the single-spoke type, was of larger diameter than that fitted to the DS. This was necessary because the car did not have hydraulic power steering; anyone who's driven one will know how much effort is required, especially when parking. Manual transmission called for a normal clutch pedal, and provision of a column-mounted gear lever. Many column gear change systems had a reputation for clumsy operation, and would often lock up during ratio selection, but that of the ID was perfectly smooth, light and precise. The absence of power-assisted braking meant that a conventional pedant brake pedal took the place of the DS's floor button, calling for determined effort on the part of the driver in order to stop the car in an emergency.

The ID's body panels and trim specification, apart from those differences already mentioned, was mostly identical to that of the DS. Aluminium bumpers front and rear were common to all models, as was the polished alloy door exterior handles and roof joint strip. Initially the ID's headlamp bezels were painted, along with the leading edge of the under-bumper valance, but within months of production commencing these anomalies were dropped. The ID's hydropneumatic suspension shared the same technology as that of the DS, all components being common to both models. Whereas the DS's hydraulic system was equipped with a belt-driven, seven piston pump to cater for

suspension, steering, gear selection and braking, that of the ID required only a single-cylinder reciprocating pump, driven by an eccentric on the camshaft.

First shown in the autumn of 1956, the ID19 did not arrive in dealer showrooms until May 1957. Two cars were featured at the Salon, both wearing bold paint schemes, one a tropical blue, the other vivid orange, as if to demonstrate the model's youthful *avant-garde* image. Both were finished to Luxe specification although a marginally more expensive Confort model was available with materials of slightly better quality. The ID19 appealed to those customers unwilling to pay the price demanded for the DS with all its complexities; even with a reduced level of trim (compared to the DS), the ID lacked nothing in character which it inherited from its sister car, and was still far more technologically advanced than its contemporaries.

Despite the massive surge of orders following the DS's introduction, the ID19 ultimately attracted more customers. Few owners bothered about the heavy steering and need to change gear manually; neither were they unhappy about the car's conventional braking. Nor did the slower performance seem to matter as the comfort and ride quality more than compensated for any lethargy in reaching a slightly lower top speed. Garage mechanics were often happier servicing the ID, having become used to the *Traction Avant*: the ID19, therefore, largely supplanted that model and,

once established, the *Traction* slipped quietly from the catalogue.

With the demise of the *Traction* in 1957, Citroën did make one concession to those customers who wanted a large car devoid of anything but the most essential equipment and for whom, therefore, even the ID19 in Luxe trim was too luxurious. Citroën made available. The Normale - what would today be known as a lead-in model - was an ID pared of every accessory in order to achieve a price of 860,000 francs, ten per cent less than that of the Luxe. Devoid of a heater, clock and ashtrays - goodness knows where the Gauloise stubs ended up - the Normale was also denied separate and reclining seats, the bench seat being upholstered in blue cloth. Minimalism extended to light beige plastic covered door panels, a sun visor for the driver only, an absence of armrests and all brightwork, apart from aluminium bumpers, boot hinges and base metal door handles. Under the bonnet, which, like taxi versions of the ID19, was made from steel rather than aluminium to facilitate easy repair, the *Traction Avant's* 11D 62bhp engine afforded barely adequate power. The Normale was available only in black and, looking very forlorn in its spartan attire, it's hardly surprising that only 390 sold between October 1957 and early 1960 when the model was withdrawn.

continued page 70

ID19s (epitomised here by Paul Chapman's 1962 car) can be identified by their small hub caps and absence of front direction indicator bezels. Interior styling was more conventional than that of the DS inasmuch that a more traditional dashboard was fitted. (Courtesy Brian Drummond)

Compare the DS indicator housing with that shown in the photograph below. (Author's collection)

French-built ID models had dark-coloured plastic rear indicator housings. (Author's collection)

This close-up view of the ID19 front wing assembly shows the car's more basic exterior trim detail. (Author's collection)

CITROËN iD 19

Hydropneumatique

Citroën's publicity material for the ID19 was particularly adventurous: who could fail to be impressed by such artistry? (Brian Chandler collection)

ID19s on the production line at Javel. Note the chevron-emblazoned protection covers fitted to the door panels, each carrying the letter D or G according to whether it was the right or left side of the car. The painted headlamp bezels amd small wheel centre covers indicate that the leading car is a very early ID19. (Courtesy Citroën)

The ID's dashboard styling. Evident is the pendant clutch pedal, parking brake lever, and suspension height control. IDs had plastic interior door handles and window winders. (Courtesy Citroën)

Citroën went to great lengths to explain the simplicity of the DS's construction (in this instance an ID19). One assumes that, having removed the doors and wing panels with nothing more sophisticated than a screwdriver and spanner, the family will reassemble the car and drive away … (Brian Chandler collection)

sure.

This delightfully evocative publicity picture combines the ID19's sophistication with chic fashion. (Brian Chandler collection)

NEW LOOK: MORE POWER; GREATER REFINEMENT

When it was introduced in 1955 Citroën claimed that the DS was two years ahead of its time. As it happened, this statement was too modest by far, and seven years later when the first styling changes were made, it was still way ahead of current design trends. In engineering terms, too, it remained technically superior to most other marques.

Many of the DS's specification changes were simultaneously applied to the ID models, although delayed in some circumstances. As far as the ID was concerned early modifications affected items of trim and the car's interior: larger hubcaps rather than the cheap-looking centre wheel plugs improved appearance, and the painted headlamps rims were discarded in favour of chrome; rectangular rear reflectors replaced the flimsy-looking round types that would have been more appropriate on a VeloSolex (moped). Inside, ID models were treated to some rationalisation of fabrics; Luxe versions received Nylon Hélanca, and jersey cloth was specified for Confort models.

Having decided to drive her ID19 along a muddy track, this young lady demonstrates the dexterity and versatility of her Citroën by raising the suspension and continuing her journey when other cars would have become bogged down. (Brian Chandler collection)

When the Luxe model benefited from the addition of armrests for rear passengers, the Confort received twin windscreen washers, footwell air vents, and a courtesy mirror for the front passenger. An arguably insignificant departure from originality on DS models was moving the wind-up clock from the face of the ashtray to within the speedometer binnacle, where it became electrically operated. ID Confort versions (not Luxe) were also provided with a clock, initially positioned on the right-hand side of the instrument binnacle immediately beneath the speedometer, but repositioned outside the binnacle.

During the early part of 1958 the ID's braking system was modified to allow for more urgent stopping in the event of an emergency. A valve in the master cylinder opened when the piston was fully activated under heavy braking to allow hydraulic fluid from the pressurised suspension system to assist operation of front and rear brakes. Not entirely successful -

Seven years after introduction the DS received a styling facelift. Compare the frontal detail of the ID19 pictured on an autumnal day (left) with the new face of the DS (above). Immediately apparent is the revised nose treatment with modified bumpers, fitted with overriders, and a smooth underside. (Courtesy Citroën)

especially when brakes were sticking due to limited use, were worn, or when hydraulic pressure was low - the system was again modified in 1962. The load sensitive pedal device was abandoned in favour of a valve arrangement which introduced the slightest delay in application of the rear brakes, a system

A year before the DS's exterior styling was modified Citroën revised the interior. This is the two-tone dashboard as introduced in the autumn of 1961. ID19 dashboards remained largely unchanged. (Brian Chandler collection)

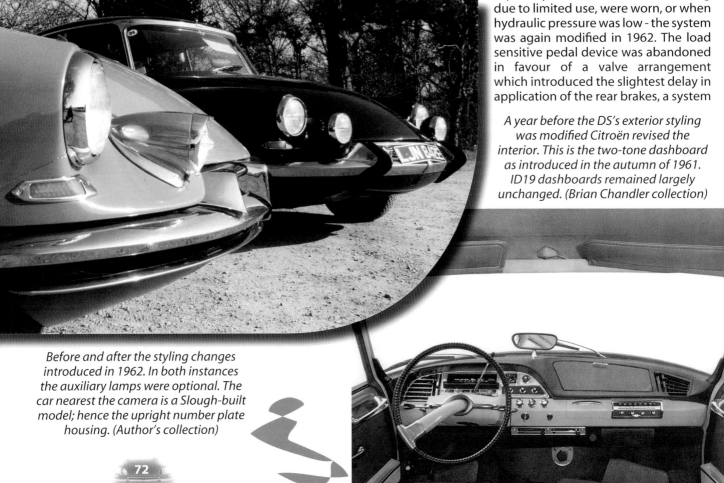

Before and after the styling changes introduced in 1962. In both instances the auxiliary lamps were optional. The car nearest the camera is a Slough-built model; hence the upright number plate housing. (Author's collection)

A post 1963 DS styling showing to good effect the modified nose treatment. This publicity illustration demonstrates Citroën's liking for industrial settings. (Brian Chandler collection)

Against a quintessentially Norman background this DS makes a fine picture. The boot space of a DS may not appear particularly capacious from the outside, but it could swallow an impressive amount of luggage. (Brian Chandler collection)

which remained on successive models for a number of years, including the XM which was discontinued in 2000. A significant change to the DS's electrical system was made in July 1959 when the rather odd twin coil ignition was abandoned in favour of a regular distributor.

For the 1960 model year both the ID and DS models received slightly restyled and longer rear wings, resulting in removal of the elongated reflector housings designed to camouflage the wings' truncated shape. The revised wing shape is most evident when early and later models are seen together; the latter type wing (retained until the end of production) extending a few millimetres from the rear edge of the boot lid. There were other modifications: mercifully, 12-volt electrics replaced the glow-worm 6-volt system which was susceptible to failure when starting in icy weather. It really is amazing that an otherwise advanced and innovative car was allowed to depend on such an antiquated system, although it has to be said that Citroën wasn't alone in this respect ...

In time for the 1962 model year the DS was blessed with a new facia and

So as not to leave the ID19 out of the domestic scene, its boot, too, is laden with luggage in this rather contrived scene. Note the styling differences between this car and the DS in the previous illustration. Small hub caps and plastic rear indicators were fitted to ID19s. (Brian Chandler collection)

instrumentation, the design departing a little from Bertoni's original and futuristic essay, although in no way could it be considered conventional. Instantly recognisable as Citroën orientated, the facia, still Bertoni styled, was largely formed from steel pressing clad in vinyl, with considerably less

reliance on plastic. Instrument layout was similar to that of its predecessor but switchgear appeared to be randomly scattered, although there was, in fact, some logic to the layout. ID saloons were not affected and retained the original design until 1969.

By far the most striking change

Citroën is renowned for some particularly artistic publicity material, as demonstrated by this emotive setting. Only the Goddess (actually an ID19) could complement such a tender scene. (Brian Chandler collection)

With its front-wheel drive and hydropneumatic suspension, the DS proved itself over all terrain. Look carefully at the front of the car and the air intakes beneath the headlamps can be seen. (Brian Chandler collection)

This scene of blissful domesticity was aimed at the American market. The car, in this instance a DS Pallas, is furnished with pod-type indicators, along with auxiliary driving lamps. (Courtesy Citroën)

Georges Simenon's Inspector Maigret is more usually associated with the Traction Avant, but here he is, played by Rupert Davies, standing alongside an ID19, Lapointe (Neville Jason) at the wheel. (Courtesy BBC)

to DS and ID styling to date was revision of the car's frontal shape in the autumn of 1962. Post 1962 cars were more aerodynamic, courtesy of new bumpers with shock-absorbing rubber overriders, the overall shape achieving a sleeker stance. The changes were not purely cosmetic but were introduced to provide more efficient under-bonnet cooling, eliminating the need for the wing-top cheese graters on DS variants. The design changes brought a new and more efficient underskirt to improve airflow beneath the car; the front apron was extended rearward and featured a single wide intake for radiator cooling, and two narrow ones for directing air to the inboard front brakes. Wings (minus their tell-tale headlamp indicators) were redesigned with slots beneath the headlamps to scoop fresh air for the car's heating and ventilation. The revisions brought about improved performance, the top speed of the DS rising to 99mph (160kph), an increase of approximately 8mph (13kph).

Nor were the styling changes introduced as a marketing ploy to stimulate sales. Behind-the-scenes at Javel there had been some pressure from the management to severely overhaul the car's design by lowering the roofline and adding extra rake to the windscreen. The designers, along with marketing personnel, were adamant that redesigning to this extent was unnecessary and would be unproductive, and fought hard to retain the car's original styling as far as possible. The changes that were implemented reflected the limit to which the design team was prepared to bend, and then only in the interest of advancing styling trends. What might have resulted if management had had its way?

CHAPTER FIVE

THE CHAPRON AFFAIR

Henri Chapron was among France's premier coachbuilders. The firm was commissioned by the Elysée Palace to build this presidential Décapotable; the car was based on the Traction Avant *15 Six H platform incorporating self-levelling rear suspension. (Author's collection)*

Henri Chapron was amongst France's most prolific coachbuilders, and his work encompassed not only Citroën but all the great car manufacturers such as Ballot, Bentley, Chénard-Walcker, Delage, Delahaye, Georges Irat, Hispano-Suiza, Hotchkiss, Panhard, Rolls-Royce, Salmson, and Talbot. Chapron's designs and quality coachwork were held in such high esteem that they influenced the French coachbuilding industry - discernible in nearly all bespoke bodies, regardless of designer/constructor - over three decades, up until the outbreak of war in 1939.

Like so many bespoke coachbuilders Henri Chapron could easily have gone out of business at the onset of WW2. Instead he left Paris to maintain a vehicle body repair workshop at Nouan-le-Fuzelier, 60 kilometres south of Orléans, returning to Levallois after hostilities had ceased to resume his coachbuilding activities. The move, in the 1930s, toward the unitary construction method of car building contributed to a large extent to the decline of the specialist coachbuilding industry. For Chapron, though, there was salvation inasmuch that he had experience of producing custom coachwork on Citroën's *Traction Avant* platforms, the grandest being a Presidential cabriolet based on the 15 Six H model. Indeed, Chapron built several state cars on a variety of chassis, including the Talbot-Lago, and completed several special commissions for Peugeot and Renault. During the early post war years Chapron was responsible for most of

Delahaye's production on 135 and 235 chassis types, along with Salmsons and Talbots.

Chapron's affair with the DS began in 1955 when he witnessed the car's unveiling at the Paris Salon. He was so impressed with the vehicle that he immediately vowed to build a convertible example, an exercise fraught with difficulty. Within the French motor industry the name of Henri Chapron was lionized, which is why it's surprising that Citroën was unwilling to sell the coachbuilder a platform on which to build his cabriolet. Whether such a convertible - or *Décapotable* - was intended for Chapron's personal use, or as a commission for a customer, matters not. What is important is that Chapron, in order to produce a convertible *Déesse*, was forced to buy a new DS saloon from a local Citroën dealer, remove the body and undertake the necessary chassis modifications before clothing it in his own four-seater coachwork. The process, which involved strengthening the chassis and lengthening the front doors by 4in (10cm), took some time, but when the car was finished and displayed by the coachbuilder in 1958 it generated a vast amount of interest.

The reason that Citroën did not want to supply Chapron with a DS platform was that the company had planned to market and construct a cabriolet of its own, the styling having been undertaken by Flaminio Bertoni during the DS saloon's gestation period. Ironically, Citroën had already commissioned Bertoni to prepare the Prestige, which was displayed for the first time at the 1958 Paris Salon, where it shared the spotlight with Chapron's cabriolet.

Citroën's intention to market a cabriolet stems from the early 1950s. Bertoni's proposals carry a 1954 date, and both two and four-seater versions were projected, some sketches retaining the overall DS theme whilst others depict a more radical image with revised frontal and tail treatment. One particular arrangement illustrates a four-seater cabriolet with a straight-through swage line, finishing in a tail reminiscent of the yet to materialise ID Break, and as seen on Giovanni Michelotti's Triumph Herald, the prototype of which appeared at the end of 1957.

Had Citroën's design team not been preoccupied with the early problems associated with the DS, and introduction of the ID, there's every reason to believe that a cabriolet derivative of the *Déesse* would have appeared within a couple of years or so of the saloon's debut. Because of the tooling that would have been

necessary, together with a higher price to take into account not only its labour intensive construction but also its undoubted desirability, Citroën's marketing department would have had little idea of what the potential demand for a cabriolet might be. It's easy, therefore, to appreciate why three years after the DS's introduction the company was reluctant to embark upon such a costly exercise.

Henri Chapron's cabriolet, known as *La Croisette*, used a fussy arrangement to blank the rear doors, and retaining the standard rear wing, and the provision of front quarterlights gave it a heavy appearance. The second cabriolet built by Chapron dispensed with the quarterlights and a blanking strip helped disguise the fact that the rear doors had been left in place. By 1959 an altogether sleeker machine appeared as a purpose-built 2+2, with a single rear wing extending from the B pillar and a cut-out to facilitate wheel changing. Known as *Le Caddy*, this was the definitive Chapron cabriolet that set a design standard with which Citroën agreed. To date Chapron had built some twenty-five DS cabriolets, all of which were converted from saloons bought complete from Citroën, and finished to an extremely high standard commensurate with the coachbuilder's art.

Henri Chapron's fine reputation, and the fact that a demand existed for the *Décapotable* (even if it was rather limited), persuaded Citroën to adopt the cabriolet as a catalogue model, available to special order only. Citroën was adamant that in commissioning

Chapron to build the *Décapotable*, the coachbuilder would have to comply with Bertoni's styling arrangement. The result of this agreement appeared at a specially convened press launch in September 1960, one month ahead of the Paris Salon. What journalists saw was a magnificent vehicle, built and appointed to the highest quality, and reminiscent of the Grandes Routières of previous decades.

Citroën had not included a cabriolet in its catalogue since before the war, and the fact that a *Décapotable* version of the DS built by Carrossiere Henri Chapron graced the manufacturer's stand at the 1960 Salon was sufficient to draw much attention. Known as Usine Cabriolets so as to distinguish the 'official' catalogue models from the coachbuilder's previous designs, the DS19 *Décapotable* became available from February 1961 with a price tag twice that of an ID19 saloon.

Within a month of the car going on sale with the originally specified 75bhp engine, the more powerful 83bhp 1911cc engine was fitted from

March 1961, so it's unlikely that any of the less powerful cars were delivered. From July the same year an ID19 version was introduced with the 66bhp engine and manual transmission, but with none of the trim paring usually associated with ID models. In February 1962 ID models were upgraded to receive the 83bhp engine, which was used to power a manual version of the DS19 from April 1963. When Citroën's new and more powerful 2175cc engine became available, this was fitted to the *Décapotable* from September 1965 in both semi-automatic and manual transmission variants, superseding the ID.

To construct the *Décapotable* Citroën delivered specially prepared DS base units to Henri Chapron's Levallois

The interest created by Chapron's DS cabriolet when unveiled at the 1958 Paris Salon convinced Citroën to award the coachbuilder a licence to build the Décapotable at Levallois. The DS19 Décapotable was announced in June 1960 with delivery beginning early in 1961. The car's attractive styling is shown here to good effect. (Courtesy Citroën)

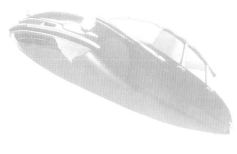

works, courtesy of Transports Bodemer, a specialist forwarding company. With each unit came a large box containing vital accessories such as window lifts, handles, and items of body furniture and trim. In essence the base units comprised running gear and drivetrain, and were suitably strengthened by having the transverse member and side longerons reinforced so that sills were marginally deeper and supported two jacking points. Unlike the saloon, which had only one jacking point, two were necessary on the *Décapotable* to properly access the rear wheels and prevent distortion of the body when lifting the car. The B-post was not fitted and the C-post was cut down to waist height to allow the coachbuilder to undertake the necessary conversion for the modified doors - 10cms (4ins) longer than the originals - and provision of the hood assembly.

When viewing the *Décapotable* it's obvious that the car's body panels aft of the front wings and scuttle differ from those of the saloon. All the conversion work was hand-crafted by Chapron's experienced personnel at Levallois, many of whom had been employed by the coachbuilder for many years. The windscreen surround was reinforced, not only to allow fitting of hood fasteners but also to support the weight of the hood when in the closed position. The hood itself (with plastic rear window opened by a zip)

was unlined, the material being either mock leather or a rubber laminated fabric. The doors, fabricated by the cut-and-shut method, were formed from two standard DS units with 3cm (1.2in) cut away from the bottom edge and fitted with double catches to reinforce rigidity. The rear section of the car was separately constructed, there being two transverse beams, and each of the rear wings were crafted in steel from two

sections, then welded to form a single body panel. The boot lid, rather than being formed from either aluminium or steel, was made from glass-fibre. Distinctive embellishments, such as the croissant-shaped rear indicators fitted to the rear quarters that hugged the hood recess, helped give the *Décapotable* its unique identity.

Other features exclusive to the *Décapotable* included the rubbing

Pictured at Malo les Bains near Dunkerque in June 2004, this Décapotable was intended for the American market, hence the distinctive front indicators. (Author's collection)

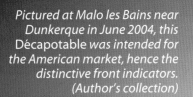

Décapotables were built to DS or ID specification according to customer option. This Belgian registered DS variant has some interesting embellishments, including a bonnet handle. The auxiliary lamps are arguably more aesthetically-pleasing than those fitted to the car in the previous picture. (Author's collection)

The Décapotable's dashboard. Beneath the ventilation control can be seen the interior light; below that, to the right, is the heating thermostat. The instruments to the left of the ventilation control and interior lamp are non-standard items, fitted retrospectively. (Author's collection)

With hood raised the interior of the Décapotable is draught-free and cosy. The car's rear indicators are triangular shaped, fitted to the top of the wings immediately aft of the hood. (Courtesy Tony Stokoe/Brian Scott-Quinn)

strips along the sides of the car. The rear bumper assemblies are also different and have extended side pieces designed to camouflage the slightly longer overhang compared to the standard saloon, which was necessary because of the build process. Despite the *Décapotable* being a mere 2cm longer than the saloon, Chapron's conversion was responsible for some weight gain - 45kg - mainly due to the extra strengthening required to construct the bespoke coachwork.

Time-consuming and intricate, the Chapron process was naturally expensive. Finishing the car to customer

The *Décapotable* is a rarity among DSs, much sought-after by discerning enthusiasts. This is Tony Stokoe's elegant example, one of fifty cars destined for the UK market. Note the Citroën script on the bonnet. (Courtesy Tony Stokoe/Brian Scott-Quinn)

Stephen Cooper's Décapotable at a DS enthusiasts rally. Décapotables were finished to a very high standard and incorporated the finest materials and craftsmanship. (Courtesy Tony Stokoe/Brian Scott-Quinn)

specification involved careful grinding and lead-loading of the welded seams, painting in one of fifteen colours offered, electrical installation, fitting of accessories and, finally, installation of the hood, which could be supplied with either manual or electrically powered operation.

A total of 1365 *Décapotables* were produced between 1960 and 1971, although a number - believed to be three - were subsequently built as special commissions, the last delivered in 1978 and constructed on a 1974 DS23 chassis to the order of the late Alan Clark, whose diverse collection of cars included a 2CV and several Bentleys and Rolls-Royces. Those cars built subsequent to September 1967 received the new look when the

frontal styling of all the D models was radically changed (see later chapter) to incorporate modified wings with twin faired-in headlamps. Cars having the revised styling received the DS21 115bhp engine, and, from September 1969, the 139bhp unit in both manual and semi-automatic variants.

Compared to the total number of DS and derivative models built, Henri Chapron's *Décapotables* are somewhat rare and so extremely collectable. Right-hand drive examples are uncommon, with only fifty destined for UK customers. The whole subject of *Décapotable* production is complicated because early examples were constructed on the DS saloon platform. When the ID version was announced powered braking was

standardised but customers could opt for power steering. Between 1964 and 1971 cars were built on the ID Break platform (the Break is discussed in a later chapter) and, subsequent to 1971, construction reverted to use of the DS saloon base unit.

Always luxuriously appointed, Chapron *Décapotables* were specified with hide upholstery, deep pile carpeting, and a superb finish. Whilst leather was the usual choice, Chapron was happy to comply with individual customer requirements. Fully reclining front seats differed from those usually found on saloon versions and tipped forward to give access to the rear bench, which was necessarily restricted in depth and width owing to the hood's folding mechanism.

Throughout production there were numerous minor modifications, such as adoption of DS Pallas indicator surrounds in 1964. Other DS Pallas equipment fitted to the *Décapotable* included auxiliary driving lamps and

continued page 86

No more than 1365 DS Décapotables were built, not counting those cars independently designed and constructed by Chapron. (Courtesy Tony Stokoe/Brian Scott-Quinn)

Joe Judt at the wheel of his Décapotable with L. J. K. Setright alongside. The occasion is the filming of an episode of the BBC programme The Car's the Star in 1994 after the car had been resprayed to its present colour. (Author's collection)

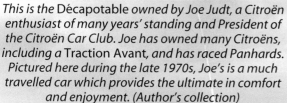

This is the Décapotable owned by Joe Judt, a Citroën enthusiast of many years' standing and President of the Citroën Car Club. Joe has owned many Citroëns, including a Traction Avant, and has raced Panhards. Pictured here during the late 1970s, Joe's is a much travelled car which provides the ultimate in comfort and enjoyment. (Author's collection)

Chapron produced a small number of Décapotables *with hard tops, this being a late example with twin headlamps. (Courtesy Rodney Cremin)*

Chapron produced the exclusive Caddy, seen here with faired-in headlamps. The rear styling is of interest as it differs to that of the official Citroën model. (Courtesy Rodney Cremin)

seats, along with a black steering wheel. Facia design was similar to that of the DS saloon, a slight change occurring after September 1968 when the lower dash panel was painted in body colour in preference to the usual grey.

Chapron production peaked in 1963 when 245 cars were delivered; 212 and 162 were supplied in 1962 and 1961 respectively. In 1964 output declined to 184 vehicles, falling again to 130 the following year. This increased slightly in 1966 with 136 cars, though only 91 were sold in 1967. Renewed interest in 1968 - probably because of revised styling - resulted in 95 cabrios being sold, but then it was downhill all the way: 47 orders were received in 1969, 40 in 1970, and a mere 19 in 1971. Of the 1365 cars officially built, 112 were constructed as ID19s and 483 as DS21s. By far the most popular were those based on the DS19, of which there were 770.

For those fortunate few enthusiasts who own a *Décapotable*, the car really does give a unique driving experience. The Chapron cabriolet appears equally handsome with its hood raised or lowered. In inclement weather the hood allows quiet and comfortable draught-free motoring, the large rear window offering particularly good visibility. Hood up or down, the *Décapotable* is the epitome of driving pleasure; an exquisite motor car, coupled with Citroën's advanced technology and superbly compliant suspension.

In addition to producing the Usine Cabriolets for Citroën, Chapron continued to build a variety of customised DSs, some as cabriolets

- a four-seater marketed as the Palm Beach and distinguishable by its retractable rear quarter windows - and others as a fixed head coupé - the Le Paris with a body style reminiscent of some Chapron Renault commissions. Built in low numbers this design was superseded by the Concorde with its more aesthetic styling and clean rear wing arrangement instead of the visible panel join. From 1965 Chapron restyled the rear wings to give a raised profile, the straight-through design more in keeping with some of Bertoni's original sketches. Among the models so equipped was the Le Léman, a true sports coupé with distinctive elegance.

Arguably less successful than some of his earlier designs was the Lorraine, a four-door saloon with extended boot and straight-through swage line that gave it a heavy appearance. Similar, but with interior appointments that would not have been out of place on a Rolls-Royce was the Majesty, a car intended for the most discerning clientele.

Henri Chapron died on 14th May 1978. His brilliant coachbuilding career spanned seventy-nine years, seven of which were spent in military service. For a few years Henri's widow carried on restoring high quality cars at Levallois, but in January 1986 the premises were sold at auction. On the site today stands a modern office block.

Over the last twenty years or so a number of DS saloons have been converted to cabriolets with mixed results. At best proper attention has been paid to strengthening the DS or ID platform, and in a number of cases the Break chassis has been

Top left: This is a later version of the Dandy; note the styling differences of the car in the previous photograph. (Courtesy Rodney Cremin)

Bottom left: From 1965 Chapron produced the distinctive and luxuriously equipped coupé Le Léman *as a 5/6 seater. (Courtesy Rodney Cremin)*

used. Careful restructuring of the bodyshell has resulted in a car with the *Décapotable's* correct dimensions and interior furnishings, although such cars could never be classed or sold as a genuine Chapron. At worst roofs have been removed from saloons with scant attention paid to reinforcing the platform. Whenever a *Décapotable* is offered for sale it is essential that the car's provenance is checked to ascertain that it is, indeed, one of the few genuine Chapron cars that survive.

The most prestigious of all DS-based Chaprons was the Majesty. Fully equipped and superbly appointed, this was also the most exclusive of models. (Courtesy Rodney Cremin)

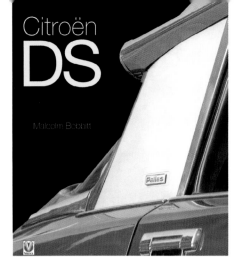

Citroën
DS

Malcolm Bobbitt

CHAPTER SIX

ON SAFARI

Estate cars, breaks, station wagons, town & country cars, shooting brakes - call them what you will - have, for years enjoyed widespread popularity with growing families and business customers alike. Station wagons were a familiar sight on American roads in the late 1930s, especially those with 'woody' type bodies.

The estate car trend did not arrive in Britain and mainland Europe until the early 1950s. It was in the wake of World War 2 that conversions on vehicles such as the Vauxhall E-Type and Ford Zephyr first began, courtesy of coachbuilders like Friary Motors of Basingstoke, Martin Walter of Folkestone, and Abbott of Farnham. Morris introduced the Traveller on its Minor and Oxford models, as did Austin with the Countryman, and other manufacturers followed suit, such as Standard, which offered estate versions of different models.

European car makers had also spotted the potential for station wagon derivatives of their mainstream models. Usually known as 'breaks', these vehicles had vast amounts of interior space and proved ideal as touring machines in which all but the proverbial kitchen sink could be accommodated. Renault had successfully produced the *Colorale* in 1950, which remained in production until the *Domaine*, a development of the *Frégate*, arrived in 1956. Peugeot, too, introduced an estate car, a derivative of the 203 which went on sale in 1950, and Panhard eventually devised a break based on the PL17. Simca, with its Ford-based Vedette, not surprisingly progressed the big station wagon theme with the Marley for 1956, a commodious machine reflecting American styling and ethos. In similar vein to the '56 Plymouth Suburban Wagon, the Marley featured an integral roof rack along with a split tail gate which gave access to the 1.6m^3 flat floor loading area with a 500kg payload. Elsewhere, Fiat latched on to the estate car market with a variety of vehicles, one of the more popular being the innovative 600-based Multipla, although this was hardly in the big car

Forerunner to the D-Series estate cars, the Commerciale *version of the* Traction Avant *was built on a long wheelbase and had a tailgate. At the 70th anniversary celebration to commemorate the* Traction, *there is an obvious atmosphere of* entente cordiale. *(Author's collection)*

The Commerciale *with opening tailgate. Prewar models had split tailgates. (Author's collection)*

F A M I L I A L E

An estate car variant of the DS had been proposed in 1955, but it was not until September 1958 that the model was announced, and a further year before delivery began. This publicity item for the Familiale *model clearly illustrates how capacious these cars are - but is there sufficient room also for the young girl with her dollies and pushchair? (Brian Chandler collection)*

league. From behind the Iron Curtain Skoda was producing estate versions of its early post war models.

While Citroën did not progress into the station wagon market proper immediately after the war, it did sell a derivative of the *Traction Avant* which, to all intents and purposes, was the forerunner of the utility vehicle or hatchback as we now know it. Commercial versions of the firm's cars existed in the late twenties; an opening rear door or hatch gave access to the vehicle's interior, and seats could be removed to provide increased luggage capacity.

Within four years of the *Traction Avant's* introduction, Citroën announced the *Commerciale*, built using the long-wheelbase platform of the 8-9 seater *Familiale*. The rear of the car was designed as a split hatch, the top section lifting upward while the lower section dropped to allow bulky items to be loaded into the interior, the rear seats folding flat for this purpose. To illustrate the vehicle's effectiveness an advertisement appeared portraying a wine-maker loading barrels of wine into the back of a car. Post war, the *Commerciale* was redesigned with a single rear top-hinged tailgate which opened in the style of a modern estate car; it can be safely claimed that it was this car that spearheaded the modern hatchback design.

With the introduction of the DS and ID there existed, therefore, an important and lucrative market for an estate car to outsize and out-perform all others. More than just a carry-all, such a vehicle could rely on the DS's hydropneumatic technology to accommodate the heaviest of loads without fear of the car sinking on its springs, with resultant nightmarish handling characteristics. As with the *Traction Avant Familiale*, a DS-based

D-Series estate cars acquired a variety of names: Breaks, Shooting Brakes, Station Wagons, and Safaris. Because of their commodious interiors and ability to carry impressively large loads, these cars were popular among Citroën customers throughout Europe. This example was photographed in Amsterdam in 1998. (Courtesy Bill Wolf)

estate car could be adapted to carry as many as seven or eight people, along with their luggage. Other possible roles included ambulance, freight carrier, and hearse.

The concept of a DS-based estate car had been proposed as early as 1955 when Bertoni produced a number of styling arrangements for Citroën's sales department. The theme was further developed by Pierre Franchiset, Citroën's chief body engineer, who, like several others at the *Bureau d'Etudes*, was also keen to combine with the company's sales and marketing department in developing an innovative people and load carrier. It was during the car's gestation period that prototypes were used by senior management on their travels throughout France: the vehicles displayed exemplary behaviour, with no discernible difference in performance whether loaded to capacity or empty.

It was quickly appreciated that the DS's hydropneumatics were ideally suited for carrying heavy equipment over long distances and at high speeds, the suspension remaining at a constant

height whatever the payload. Moreover, the capacity of an estate car version of the DS, its overall performance, comfort and handling, outclassed any vehicle then in production.

Using the fundamental design technology of the DS, it was a relatively straightforward task to develop an estate car derivative. The DS's long wheelbase was perfectly adequate for such a purpose, so there was no need to lengthen it, as might have been the

case with other marques. What was necessary was a tail extension, and although the estate car appears much longer than the saloon, the difference is in fact minimal at just 195mm (7.68in). The disparity in overall length was actually reduced to 152mm (5.98ins) on later cars with the revised frontal design incorporating faired-in headlamps. Because of the car's increased weight

A feature of the Break is the tailgate which lifts completely clear of the rear hatch to allow unimpeded access to the car. (Brian Chandler collection)

BREAK

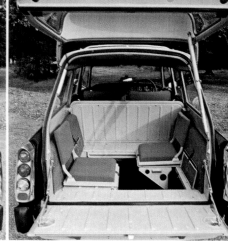

The interior of a D estate car, with and without the occasional seats in position.
(Brian Chandler collection)

According to model specification two occasional seats are to be found in the Break's rear compartment. When not in use the seats can be folded away to provide a flat loading area.
(Courtesy Brian Drummond)

(80kg (176lb) heavier than the saloon), and owing to the potential loads to be conveyed, two jacking points instead of one were positioned each side of the vehicle in order to allow it to be lifted without causing too much stress to the chassis under full load conditions. It was also necessary to incorporate wheelarches into the rear wings, again, for ease of wheel changing and jacking. A steel roof incorporating a roof rack replaced the standard fibreglass unit, and a unique feature of the car was its split tailgate arrangement which allowed unimpeded access to the car's interior.

Announced in Paris during the autumn of 1958, and going on sale a year later in readiness for the 1960 model year, the Break, as it was officially known, was partly built by Citroën at Javel and partly subcontracted to specialist coachbuilder Carrosserie de Levallois. The firm was formerly known as Faget et Varnet, a coachbuilder of some repute which, during the late 1940s, built for Renault a bonnetless taxi, much in the idiom of the modern MPV. Citroën supplied to the coachbuilder all the necessary chassis parts to construct the caisson and rear body sub-assembly, along with the tailgate structure, the sheet steel being

0.3mm (0.01in) thicker than that used on saloons.

The only body panels to differ from those of the saloon were the rear wings, which incorporated wheelarches and were square cut and elongated in accordance with the estate car's body profile. The shape of the wings was similar to those Bertoni had devised whilst preparing styling studies for a cabriolet version of the DS. Although the rear doors were identical to the saloon's, the glass was necessarily different to account for the Break's revised roofline. The car's rear lights were also redesigned to accommodate the tailgate assembly, and were incorporated into the trailing edges of the wings. The tailgate design was innovative inasmuch that the upper unit, with its large curved screen, was so hinged that when in the raised position it lifted clear of the rear hatch; the lower section cleverly dropped downward to facilitate loading of cumbersome items as well as acting as a tailboard on which to support long loads. The lower tailgate was equipped with two sets of number plates so that, when in the open position, the number was clearly displayed; a simple but nevertheless ingenious method of staying legal!

Once the coachbuilders had completed the chassis assembly and body frame it was returned to Javel where the build process was finished. There, the drivetrain, all mechanical components, remaining external panels, and electrics were fitted, and

trimming carried out according to specification.

INTERIOR APPOINTMENT

Citroén estate cars - known in the United Kingdom as Safaris, the name given to the model by the British subsidiary at Slough - were marketed in ID guise and not DS. With a massive 640kg payload, four versions became available on introduction: Break; *Commerciale*; *Familiale*, and Ambulance. Both the Break and *Familiale* were trimmed to Luxe or Confort specification according to choice, whilst the *Commerciale* was available in Luxe trim only; Ambulances were produced in Confort specification only.

Of all the estate car models Breaks were especially popular and were mostly specified with Confort trim. The Luxe, with its reduced specification and utilitarian cloth-based plastic upholstery, was too utilitarian for most customers. Confort models were better equipped with a more versatile seating arrangement. There was a choice of a front bench seat which accommodated three passengers, or separate reclining front seats; in either case both were covered in nylon Hélanca, with Jersey cloth becoming available later. Initially, Luxe-trimmed cars had a folding rear seat, whilst that on Confort models was fixed, though eventually both versions had folding rear seats. A feature common to both models was the occasional folding rear seats situated in the tail section: side-facing,

AU TRAVAIL

EN PROMENADE

6 personnes et leurs bagages

8 personnes et leurs bagages

The DS is a practical load carrier, as graphically illustrated in this publicity material. Whatever the number of passengers and size of load, the car remains at a constant ride level courtesy of hydropneumatic suspension. (Brian Chandler collection)

the narrow seats were mainly intended for children but could accommodate adults at a push.

The *Familiale* had a quite different seating configuration. Front seats were, until 1961, of the bench type, although separate reclining seats did become available subsequently. With Confort models now specified with upholstery more luxurious than the spartan Luxe type, all *Familiales* had a revised floor pan arrangement with the fuel tank moved rearward to between the wheelarches. This allowed three forward-facing folding occasional seats to be fitted between the front and rear seats to provide accommodation for seven or eight passengers, according to whether a front bench was fitted. The seating arrangement was in true limousine fashion, and with the occasional seats folded away, those rear seat passengers had ample leg room. The downside of the *Familiale* is that whilst it is an efficient people carrier, luggage space is seriously compromised when carrying a full complement of passengers.

The *Commerciale* had no pretensions to be anything other than completely utilitarian with its fixed front bench seat and folding rear seat, both of which were upholstered in hard-wearing plasticised cloth. Rear occasional seats were not provided, and with the rear seat folded away a huge load area became available.

Certainly the ideal car for traders, *Commerciales* did not always appeal to domestic users in the same way.

As Citroën's sales department had correctly predicted there was an enormous demand for D-Series estate cars. More than 4200 were sold in the first year of production, the figure rising to in excess of 4500 during the second year. Production peaked in 1967 with some 6180 examples sold, these figures not including the specialist Ambulance model.

For the first couple of years of production, engine and transmission specification mirrored that of the

Citroën Safaris received similar technical development to the saloons so that when faired-in headlamps were introduced they were fitted across the entire range of cars. All Safari estate cars had factory-fitted roof racks, and this right-hand drive example has a topical paint scheme. (Courtesy Brian Drummond)

use in mountainous regions, cars with a lower final drive became available, and from October 1964 the model range was fitted with tri-axe inner constant velocity joint driveshafts, a year in advance of on saloons. Unlike ID saloons, which were powered by the 1985cc engine, Breaks received more power courtesy of the DS21

ID saloon, though there were some variations in respect of braking, steering and suspension systems. At first all models featured the heave-ho unassisted steering of the ID saloons but were soon uprated to the powered system of the DS. While this became standard for some markets, those cars destined for the French market were modified according to option. Because estate car models were designed to carry heavier than usual loads, their braking system was similar to that on saloon models, controlled not by the ID's pendant pedal but the floor-mounted mushroom device. Additionally, brake drums (fitted with cooling fins for greater efficiency) were of increased diameter, as were brake shoes; consequently brake cylinders were also larger. The suspension was also boosted so that rear spheres were pressurised to 526psi instead of the usual 369psi, and larger diameter suspension spheres (40mm compared to 35mm) and reinforced wheel arms were fitted accordingly.

The ID19 engine fitted to the early Breaks was supplanted in March 1963 by the 83bhp 1911cc unit that powered the DS, although the original three-bearing motor survived as an

option until 1966, albeit in very limited numbers. When the new generation of five-bearing engines arrived these were immediately adopted for the entire range of Breaks, in 90bhp form rather than the 84bhp fitted to ID saloons. For

Breaks appealed to business users as well as motorists needing a large and highly functional vehicle. Unlike most estate cars the DS handled like a saloon, irrespective of the load carried. (Courtesy Tony Stokoe/Brian Scott-Quinn)

2175cc from September 1965, an improvement welcomed by owners who transported heavy loads.

Unlike the DS, Breaks and their relative ID saloons were never fitted with fully automatic Borg Warner transmission, though the semi-automatic gearbox from the DS was optional when D-Series cars received their styling facelift incorporating the new headlamp arrangement, more of which later. In such cases models were given an FH suffix; for example ID19FH. These cars, whilst popular in Britain, found little favour in France or mainland Europe in general, as they were considered too expensive and the semi-auto gearbox an unneccessary luxury. When the Break 23 was announced in September 1972 this became the ultimate estate car. With a 2347cc engine producing 124bhp, and specified with dual choke Weber carburetion or Bosch electronic fuel injection, the Break 23 would cruise at in excess of 100mph (160.9km/h) - performance difficult to better some 35 years on.

SPECIAL USE VEHICLES

What more efficient way of transporting the sick or injured than by high speed ambulance with the smoothest of rides, and ability to lower the suspension to assist patient boarding with minimum effort and stress? As an ambulance the DS Break fulfilled an important role, and was marketed as such throughout the car's entire production run, continuing after saloons were discontinued in favour of the CX.

A familiar sight on European roads, Safaris built as ambulances were widely used in the UK by the Inter-County Ambulance Service. That the DS was able to remain at a constant ride height, whatever its speed and quality of road surface, made it ideally suited to ambulance work, especially when transporting seriously ill patients, such as those with spinal injuries. The Break's voluminous interior allowed essential medical equipment to be carried, such as oxygen cylinders, and a stretcher could be stowed lengthways in the rear compartment allowing a nurse or attendant to sit alongside the patient. Completely functional, Breaks built as ambulances were designed with a number of options, which included GRP 'highline' roofs that gave increased interior space, a necessity when carrying blood transfusion apparatus. GRP roofs were supplied by specialist suppliers, coachbuilder Currus, and Patrick Petit, in particular, and were appreciated by many operators.

Ambulances were always equipped with curtains or blinds for privacy, and a 60/40 split rear seat, both sections folding to form a flat floor if required. Additionally it was possible to specify rear side-facing occasional seats - known as jump seats or strapontins - which folded flush with the floor. The majority of vehicles were fitted with separate front seats, though a bench seat was originally specified and remained optional.

More than 12,000 ambulances were built by Citroën in France and actually outsold Familiale and *Commerciale* models. When an announcement from Paris indicated the demise of the D-Series cars there was a rush to buy up stocks of Breaks for conversion purposes, especially since an ambulance derivative of the CX had yet to make an appearance. As it happened, the CX was a rather more complex and expensive vehicle to convert; thus ambulance operators were keen to acquire as many D Breaks as possible.

In addition to Citroën-built ambulances a number of coachbuilders offered designs of their own. Among the more successful and popular were

DS ambulances were a familiar sight throughout Europe; this example is pictured in Paris during the late 1970s or early '80s. Note the 'highline' roof which was essential if a lot of equipment was to be carried, especially that for blood transfusions. (Author's collection)

those constructed by Currus which sported squarer bodies and a single, narrow rear door fitted to the passenger side of the vehicle. Currus, incidentally, had been producing coachwork for Citroën and Panhard since the 1920s and later concentrated on conversion work building ambulances, minibuses and hearses on various chassis. Following closure of the Currus factory in 1973, Petit continued producing its own design of ambulance, along with conversions undertaken by Heuliez, Fisher of Belgium, and the Dutch firm Visser.

There were, of course, many applications to which the Citroën Break was ideally suited. In particular it was a popular choice for undertakers, the car's rear compartment easily accepting a coffin, and with the suspension in the lowest position allowing it to be loaded and unloaded with maximum ease. DS hearses were marketed by Citroën in the United Kingdom but few were actually sold. As camera cars Breaks were popular with film makers,

In addition to the 12,000 or so ambulances built by Citroën, others were constructed by specialist suppliers. Note the custom coachwork and non-standard tailgate. (Author's collection)

As a special purpose vehicle the DS estate car had few, if any, rivals. Used by the BBC for outside broadcasting, the DS was universally favoured by the film industry, and in this instance is being used as a camera car. The film - L'Insoutenable - was shot in France and starred Daniel Day Lewis and Juliette Binoche. (Courtesy Phil Bray and Elizabeth Pursey)

for not only could they swallow huge amounts of equipment, the stable ride made them eminently suitable for tremor-free filming. For a number of years the BBC used Safaris for outside broadcasts, and they were a familiar sight at race meetings.

Breaks were also used for more unusual purposes, typically newspaper deliveries around London. Another unusual application was conversion to vehicle transporter, undertaken by coachbuilders Tissier or Heuliez.

As an all-purpose and highly efficient load carrier, DS Breaks, whatever the model, have few peers. Would-be rivals like the big Fords, Vauxhalls, and Volvos, and even the D's successors, lack the comfort, charisma and capacity of the D-Series cars.

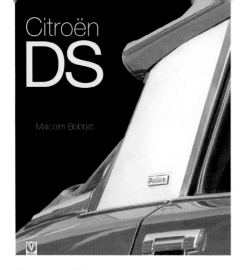

Citroën
DS

Malcolm Bobbitt

CHAPTER SEVEN
BUILT IN BRITAIN

Citroën cars were produced in the UK between 1926 and 1966. Cars assembled at the Slough factory were destined for British and Commonwealth customers. Here, a DS is seen in skeleton form at the British works. (John Reynolds collection)

It is not widely appreciated that the DS and its siblings were assembled at Slough in England, in a factory André Citroën officially opened in 1926 to much acclaim. Not only was the DS one of many models built at Slough to cater for home demand, but vehicles assembled there were exported to markets throughout the British Commonwealth.

The factory, on Slough's huge trading estate, now Slough Estates, formed an intrinsic part of Citroën Cars Limited, a wholly owned subsidiary of Automobiles Citroën which was incorporated on 27th July 1923 with a share capital of £100,000. When opened, the factory's claim to fame was that it constituted the largest British car works under a single roof, though that

did not mean it enjoyed the largest production.

The cars constructed at the factory were unique inasmuch that, whilst essentially similar to those produced in Paris, they often incorporated modifications more suited to British motorists. Those vehicles destined for export were likewise modified to suit local conditions and were highly regarded for their build quality and reliability. Cars were exported to Australia, New Zealand, and South Africa, to name but a few markets, and today surviving vehicles attract an enthusiastic following.

Another factor which made Slough cars unique was that they were equipped with a large percentage of British-sourced components, a

The DS was despatched from Paris in CKD form and assembled at Slough. A proportion of the components were sourced from British manufacturers, which gave the cars a particular identity as well as conforming to British legislation. This illustration shows part of the assembly process - the bodyshell being mated to the platform. (Author's collection)

requirement that enabled them to be built in Britain and therefore exempt from import taxation penalties. British Citroëns were delivered with Lucas electrical parts, along with wheels, radiators, bumpers, fuel tanks, exhaust systems and interior furnishings acquired from British component manufactures. Additionally, the Slough workforce included skilled carpenters who crafted the cars' wooden instrument boards, and upholsterers who trimmed and stitched hides to make seats.

Citroën, as a foreign manufacturer, was not alone in having an assembly facility in the United Kingdom: Renault had a factory at Acton in west London, and Fiat a plant in nearby Wembley. Citroën's Slough factory was no small undertaking. Located on 666 acres of land that was once used by the War Ministry as a repair depot in which to salvage military vehicles collected from throughout Europe, the contribution that the factory's output made to the British motor industry as a whole was significant. When it was opened, the factory - comprising some 696,400sq ft of floor space, together with an option on a further sixty acres of land - boasted the most modern technology then available to motor manufacturers, and up to 1939 was responsible for building nearly 29,000 vehicles. The main assembly area was confined to a huge workshop measuring 342,000sq ft, which Citroën claimed was the largest factory under one roof. During World War 2 the factory contributed to the war effort by constructing no fewer than 23,480 Canadian Military Pattern

lorries, in addition to undertaking other work such as supplying parts for tanks and aircraft. A total of 140,058 vehicles were built at the factory between 1926 and 1966, after which assembly ceased and all right-hand drive vehicles were imported to Britain from France.

In addition to rear-drive Citroëns, *Traction Avant* models, as well as 2CVs, were built at Slough. The factory was also responsible for a model unique to Britain, the *Bijou*, a 2CV clothed in a fibreglass bodyshell that made this otherwise frugal utility vehicle a more attractive proposition for British motorists, who remained unappreciative of the *Deux Chevaux* with its rugged charms and mechanical simplicity. But even the demure *Bijou*, which some said resembled a DS in miniature, failed to capture the hearts of the British people, despite its economical running costs. As history has shown, cars like the *Bijou* just could not compete with the Mini, which was officially introduced on 26th August 1959.

Ken Smith's efforts in bringing the first DS to Britain in time for its introduction in 1955 have already been related. To factory personnel engaged in building the *Traction Avant*, the Light and Big Fifteens, and Six-Cylinder models, the car, naturally, appeared radical in the extreme. Unlike in France, where production of the *Traction Avant* continued until 1957, announcement

of the DS in Britain brought *Traction* production to a halt in order to prepare Slough for building the new car.

SLOUGH PREPARES FOR THE DS

A year before the DS was introduced in France, Slough's chief of production was told he was being sent to work at the *Bureau d'Etudes*, and that he would be dividing his time between Paris and the British factory. For Ken Smith this was a welcome challenge for he was fluent in French; moreover, for a young man the opportunity was too good to miss, even if he was apprehensive about the task and responsibilities which lay before him. While he was briefed about his mission he was required to maintain total secrecy about the objectives of his work, which were to familiarise himself with the DS, advise the requirements for assembling the car in Britain, and ultimately oversee the transition of Slough's production processes.

The arrival of the DS in time for the 1955 London Motor Show signalled the beginning of a most fraught period at Slough. Production of Light and Big Fifteens ceased, along with the 15 Six H, to the dismay of loyal customers, many of whom had been contemplating replacing their existing cars with the latest model. Then, when the DS did make its dramatic appearance

at the London Show, Citroën's sales personnel, in stark contrast to their French counterparts, declined to take orders! There were simply no cars to sell whilst the Slough assembly line was dismantled and re-tooled, a massive undertaking which took eight months to complete.

Work began by ripping out assembly lines on which *Traction Avants* had been built. New technology replaced these; a suitably re-tooled production line included installation of an entirely new paint shop complete with spray booths and drying ovens capable of accommodating the DS. So that the factory was not entirely closed, assembly of the 2CV continued, albeit in moderate numbers commensurate with demand.

During this time work began on converting to right-hand drive 200 DSs that had been partially assembled in Paris. The object of the exercise was to provide essential training for assembly personnel whilst maintaining a level of output at Slough, though this was decidedly meagre. The conversion process included fitting all mechanical elements and all hydraulic components. About the latter, precious little was known, especially as strict secrecy surrounded this technology. Once the cars were mechanically complete all that was left to do was fit the body panels, which, like the bodyshells, had been prepared in primer in advance of final painting.

Conversion of the advance delivery of bodyshells was accomplished during the time it took for the tooling and body jigs required to build the DS to arrive

from Paris and be installed. Not all 200 cars were destined for customers in the United Kingdom; a little over a third were exported to Commonwealth countries. By September 1956 re-tooling was complete; initial production was painfully slow at just three cars a day, but did gradually pick up.

Slough's assembly process involved receiving from Paris pre-fabricated caissons, onto which was built the necessary superstructure. Body panels, too, were imported from France, as were engines, transmissions, all hydraulic and hydropneumatic components, and those items specific to the DS for which there was no other manufacturing source. British component manufacturers supplied the other items, which eventually were sufficient in number to meet the regulatory 51 per cent of the total which was necessary if import duty was to be avoided.

Parts from France were despatched in CKD form relative to the number of caissons delivered, although the system did not always work as well as it should. Deliveries from Paris were often incomplete, and long periods elapsed before the missing items were received. This situation obviously compromised production times and it was decided that regular trips to Paris to collect back order parts was a worthwhile exercise. Three visits a month were made to Javel in a 2CV Van. There were occasions when it was necessary to bypass the usual routine in order to complete an urgent order, and in such circumstances partially completed vehicles were cannibalised in order to

meet delivery requirements.

Production of the DS at Slough took some time to become fully established; so much so that fewer than 1000 cars (995 to be precise) rolled off the assembly line during the 1957 model year. Cars that were despatched to Citroën agents - who were often responsible for collecting their cars from the factory - were quickly sold or had been pre-ordered, despite a high price tag. At introduction the price of a DS19 was £1150 plus tax, taking it to a few shillings over £1726. This was substantially higher than the cost of a Jaguar 2.4 and 3.4, and only slightly less than the Jaguar Mark VIII and Jaguar XK150 sportscar. The DS19 cost more than the Armstrong-Siddeley Saphire, Daimler Century, Rover 90, and Humber Hawk, and was on a par with Rover's top-of-the-range 105R. There was no question about it, the DS was expensive at well above the psychological £1000 price barrier, pre-tax. Customers who could afford such a luxury car would have had to be pretty adventurous to choose a DS, despite its reputation as being highly advanced, when Jaguars (especially), Humbers and Rovers were considered status symbols.

There were a number of detail differences between the Paris and Slough DSs. Slough cars were fitted with a rectangular front number plate box so that the registration plate was fixed in an upright position in accordance with British legislation. Lucas headlamps were slightly smaller than those on French models; aluminium roofs were a standard feature, and rear indicator lenses were

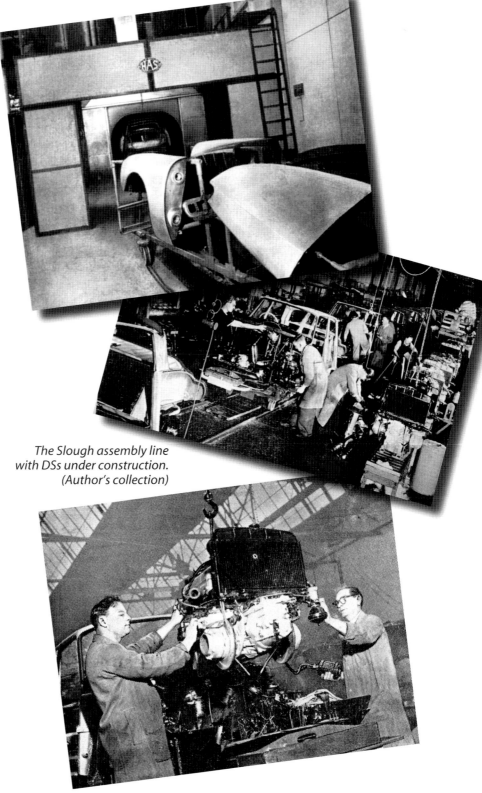

The Slough factory had to be re-tooled for DS production, an operation which called for the installation of new drying ovens. Having been commissioned, the ovens are accepting DS body panels. (Author's collection)

exposed rather than semi-concealed by the hooded trompettes. Circular rear lights replaced the rectangular types, though rear reflectors were triangular in shape. A low wattage parking lamp on the offside central pillar was a feature common to many vehicle types, allowing a light to be left on when the car was parked by the roadside at night. From the outset of production Slough cars carried 12-volt positive earth electrics, and on opening their bonnets the large oil bath type air filter was evident, a requirement for both home and export vehicles.

Slough cars also carried the Citroën script on the bonnet, on the passenger side of the car. Hide covered the car's seat facings with seat backs and door panels in leathercloth. Being of British manufacture the seats were a different style to those designed for French cars, and lacked to some extent the same support and comfort. The facia, daringly plastic for British motorists, was a mirror image of Bertoni's design seen on French models; a disappointment, possibly, to more conservative motorists who preferred the more traditional style of timber instrument board with round dials to give that essential sporting ambience. To others, Bertoni's revolutionary design was inspirational, and perfectly complemented the car's advanced engineering.

The most technically advanced DS19 must surely be that which was supplied to the Transport and Road Research Laboratory at Crowthorne in Berkshire. The car, a 1960 model, was one of a number used by the

The Slough assembly line with DSs under construction. (Author's collection)

Engine, gearbox and radiator being installed on a DS. There was some reluctance on the part of British motorists to experience the DS - an expensive car which cost as much as a Jaguar - although those who did were won over by its effortless performance and outstanding comfort. (Author's collection)

facility, a *Traction Avant* previously provided for experimental work. The Slough-built DS19 was supplied to the laboratory at a time when motorway construction was in its infancy. Britain's first stretch of motorway, the Preston bypass, which now forms part of the M6 in Lancashire, was opened in 1958. Traffic levels, and the onset of possible serious congestion, had led the Road Research Laboratory to study the feasibility of automatically controlling motor vehicles. One of the experiments concerned laying cables beneath the road surface which sent messages to an electronic 'brain' in the car. The DS19 was suitably modified by the laboratory and tests carried out manoeuvring a 'driverless' car around the Crowthorne test track for hours on end, accelerating, braking, cornering, and covering every other function in all weathers and road conditions that could be expected. Even now, in the 21st century, effective ways of remotely controlling traffic are still being sought.

The high price of the DS, along with the car's complexity, acted as deterrents to some customers - unless they had actually tried the car and experienced the smooth ride, technical wizardry, and spaceship looks - whereupon they were smitten! £1726 for a car was a lot of money, and certainly in the luxury bracket. For exactly the same reasons that a simpler DS was proposed for the French market, there was every reason to believe that a less expensive (cheaper is such a vulgar word in the motor trade!) version of the car, with less reliance on hydraulic wizardry,

would entice more British customers to the marque. With the introduction of the ID19 in France, Slough lost no time developing a corresponding model designed to appeal to British drivers, in particular the Humber, Jaguar, Riley, Rover, and Wolseley brigades.

Externally it was difficult to distinguish a Slough DS19 from a Slough ID19 when it went on sale in March 1958, by which time the less complex model had been in production in France for some eighteen months. Immediate giveaways to the model's identity were the badging, the Citroën script on the bonnet and chevrons on the boot lid being chrome rather than gilt, and the body colour painted C pillar panel, which on DS models was of bright finish. Unlike their French cousins, Slough ID19s were fitted with full-size wheel embellishers, and the same level of external trim was extended to both models. Likewise, the DS and ID were finished to the same high standard of paintwork, a two-tone arrangement optional, the shade of roof contrasting with body colours.

Open the doors of a Slough ID19, marketed as the ID19 de Luxe in the essence of British fashion, and it was obvious that both cars were trimmed alike, with Connolly or Bridge of Weir hide seat facings and leathercloth elsewhere, as on the DS. Here was that distinctive opulence so characteristic of certain British cars. The seats, constructed and trimmed within the factory, were extremely comfortable although with shorter cushions than those on French vehicles. Ashtrays were fitted into the back of the front

seats for the convenience of rear passengers. Slough IDs were fitted with a different type of dashboard to that of the DS: designed to appeal to British taste, they, like those made for the *Traction Avant*, were crafted from walnut and then polished by skilled carpenters, some of whom had worked at the factory for years. Early IDs were fitted with instruments similar in style to those used on the DS, but these were quickly changed to round dials made by Smiths Industries. Standard equipment comprised a clock, ammeter, fuel gauge, and speedometer with both odometer and mileometer; switches positioned along the lower edge of the facia operated a wind-back self-cancelling direction indicator, windscreen wiper, windscreen washer, parking light, interior lights, and the heating and ventilation fan. The open glovebox design changed to one with a drop-down lid.

The ID19 de Luxe went on sale at £998 plus tax, which took the price to £1498-7s-0d, placing it on a par with the Jaguar 2.4 saloon, Riley Two-point-Six, and Rover 75 and 90. It offered superlative comfort, courtesy of a suspension shared with the DS, though performance was adequate rather than impressive. The ID's engine was basically similar to that of the DS but with reduced output because of a lower compression ratio for economy. The four-speed manual transmission provided relaxed cruising speeds in top gear, although towns and hilly areas took their toll, requiring selective use of the gearbox in order to make decent progress.

This photograph was taken during the late 1960s outside Portfield Garage near Christchurch in Hampshire. The car on the extreme right is one of the first to feature the modified styling introduced for 1968, by which time the Slough factory had closed. The car parked beneath the canopy is a Slough-built vehicle of pre-1963 vintage. Adjacent to it is a car dating from around the time of the factory's closure, so is most likely to be Paris-built. The other cars in the picture are a Citroën Dyane, Vauxhall Victor and, almost out of view, a Volvo. Other points of interest in this photo include the contemporary Citroën logos fitted to the workshop facia and canopy above the distinctively styled National petrol pumps, the diamond-shape clock above the showroom entrance (showing a time of twenty minutes past six), and the Michelin advertisement for ZX tyres. (Courtesy Martin Thomas)

An early Slough DS19 which, like a lot of British-built examples, has a dual colour scheme. Note the gear selector visible at the top of the steering column. (Courtesy Andy Burnett)

Externally it's difficult to tell apart a British DS19 and ID. The car in these pictures is an ID19; one of the oldest surviving of the Slough Ds, it once served as a Citroën Cars press and publicity vehicle. The script on the bonnet was specific to Slough models, which were required to conform to UK legislation, thus calling for the registration plate to be mounted upright. Unlike French IDs, Slough versions received full-size hub caps. (Author's collection)

Despite the steering being heavy at low speeds, especially when parking, it was sufficiently light once under way. Gear changing wasn't a problem, the column change being light and positive in use, unlike that on some cars which had a tendency to lock up or perform clumsily. Nor was braking a problem, the front discs having ample stopping power, even without the DS's power operation. Like Jaguar, Riley, and Rover, the ID19 was a professional person's car, the choice of doctors, solicitors, bank managers, and successful businesspeople.

Having originally been denied the DS's hydraulically power-assisted braking, this eventually became available on Slough IDs from 1961; the car's steering, too, came in for some modification from 1963 when the DS's power-operated system became optional. From 1962 both the ID19 and DS19 received the same frontal styling modifications as the French cars, except that the rectangular number plate box stayed the same in accordance with UK legislation. The suspension height control lever remained on the left-hand side of the vehicle, which entailed the driver having to dive across the car (or allow a passenger to operate the lever) when it was necessary to adjust the vehicle's ground clearance. From October 1962 the lever on right-hand drive cars was relocated to the driver's side via a linkage running across the car.

SLOUGH SAFARIS
Eighteen months after the ID19 Saloon

continued page 111

British market ID19 dashboards were designed and fabricated within the Slough factory. Crafted from wood and with dedicated instrumentation, this detail is much admired by marque enthusiasts. (Courtesy Brian Drummond)

Slough cars were fitted with UK-sourced external trim items. Compare the rear indicator design with the French equivalent shown elsewhere. (Author's collection)

The interior of a Slough-built ID19 showing hide upholstery and wooden dashboard. (Courtesy Dave Ashworth)

Slough cars, such as this ID19, received similar styling modifications to their French siblings. (Courtesy Brian Drummond)

Citroën

Below & right: These two publicity pieces are delightful in the degree of artistic licence that they take. Were frontal styling and rear wings ever so elongated? By the time this publicity material appeared technical modifications to the car included powered braking on the ID19. (Author's collection)

 A Citroen DS is the ultimate in motoring

All the unique and basic features of the Citroen shown on the previous pages are

incorporated in the Citroen iD—front-wheel drive, air-suspension, powered braking etc. The iD is

for those who prefer a manually controlled gearbox with conventional clutch and driving controls.

Reliability, comfort, safety, performance and economical running

carried to the highest degree make the iD unique for value.

unique

ROEN iD

made its British debut Slough unveiled an Anglo Saxon version of the ID19 Break priced at £1308, which, with purchase tax, rose to £1854. This was the Citroën Safari in Britain, quite the largest and most accommodating vehicle of its type.

The Safari - introduced in September 1959 for the 1960 model year - was first sold as an estate car with side-facing folding occasional seats in the rear compartment. For the 1964 model year the Tourmaster was introduced, a version akin to the *Familiale* as sold in France. Tourmasters failed to attract even modest numbers of British customers due to a hefty price tag; a shade under £2000 with tax, £300 more than the contemporary Safari, which had, by then, been reduced to £1699 with tax. In Britain the Safari and Tourmaster were in the luxury bracket, on a price par with the Rolls-Royce-powered Vanden Plas Princess R, and even out-pricing Rover saloons, the Daimler 2½ litre V8, Jaguar 3.8 and E-type, and Humber's big estate cars. For the ultimate Safari there was always the Countryman conversion which was supplied to special order by

Pictured in London's King's Road, this early Slough Safari makes a fine contrast to the Austin Westminster parked behind it, and the Bedford van facing into the turning by Martins Bank. Safaris, like the Slough saloons, were fitted with full-size wheel trims. (Courtesy Citroën)

A Slough car being road tested under conditions that would have severely challenged other cars. (John Reynolds collection)

The Safari estate car was built at Slough, going on sale in September 1959 for £1854, including purchase tax. An expensive car, it had few rivals. Shown here is a post 1963 example. (Author's collection)

An eight-seater or eight feet of completely flat floor . . .

**The unique
CITROEN SAFARI**

A Safari leaving the Slough factory, followed by two saloons. It was customary for Home Counties Citroën dealers to collect cars direct from the factory, and here the Safari is seen ready to be driven away once the necessary paperwork has been completed. (Courtesy Citroën)

coachbuilder Harold Radford, purveyor of distinctive and specially equipped cars, such as the Rolls-Royce Silver Cloud and Bentley S, to discerning customers intent on travelling in unique style.

Safaris were given identical paint colour options to saloons and, unlike French-built vehicles which had roofs and rear quarters finished in grey, were supplied in the chosen body colour throughout, unless a two-tone scheme had been ordered. Slough Safaris were trimmed to the same high standard as saloons but differed mechanically by having the DS's power-assisted braking operated via the mushroom pedal. It was 1962 before power

Dan Fletcher driving away from a Brittany Ferries vessel in his 1964 Safari after a visit to France. As can be seen, the car easily accommodates five or more passengers and their luggage. (Courtesy Dan Fletcher/Brittany Ferries)

The DS was marketed to the funeral trade which preferred more conventional vehicles. In fact, the Safari made an ideal hearse because its adjustable suspension made loading and unloading of coffins easier. (Author's collection)

Unique---
the CITROEN Cortège

A factory-built hearse with following cars in the same

MODERN, DISTINGUISHED STYLE

The Pallas did not originally feature in the British catalogue, and it was 1965 before a Slough version became available. Marketed with either semi-automatic or manual transmission, this was the most luxurious of the Slough saloons, priced at a fraction under £2000. Note the special Pallas wheel trims and dedicated badging on the C-pillar. (Courtesy Citroën)

steering became optional, and the cars were never fitted with semi-automatic transmission.

The Safari formed the basis for a number of special vehicles supplied by Slough, including ambulances and hearses, though never in anything but small numbers compared to those in use in mainland Europe.

LUXURY IN THE FULLEST SENSE

Of all the Slough DSs it was the *Pallas* which was the most luxurious. British customers hoping to order a *Pallas* from Slough when that model became available in France in 1964 were to be disappointed, as it was not included in the UK catalogue. It was to be another year, and after introduction of the DS21, before a *Pallas* was offered, a truly luxury car priced at £1977 which, with tax, put it in the £2000 price bracket. Semi-automatic and manual transmission versions of the car were marketed, both similarly priced. Externally, the cars were identified by rubbing strips along the lower sections of the doors and rear wings, bright stainless-steel C-pillars, distinctive wheel embellishers. and auxiliary driving lamps. Internally, the *Pallas* received deeply-cushioned, hide-trimmed seats with bolster-type headrests and a facia the twin of the French version except that the instrument panel looked more attractive with Smiths Industries dials.

A *Pallas* version of the DS19 had not been made available as Slough had introduced the DW in 1963 which, in effect, was a DS19 with manual transmission; in France the car was marketed as the DS19M. Slough had

in fact stolen a lead over the French by developing a manual version of the DS19 as early as 1961, the prototype of which was evaluated by Buckinghamshire Constabulary. Evaluated is, perhaps, too ambitious a description; even though Citroën hoped that the exercise might result in the model being commissioned for patrol and pursuit duties, it actually became the Chief Constable's personal car ...

Clearly the DW was the answer to those customers who wanted DS styling and technological innovation, but who were reticent about automatic or semi-automatic transmission. *Autocar* magazine was full of praise for the car, finding its performance - courtesy of the four-speed, all-synchromesh gearbox - quite exhilarating: "... the sweetest mechanically as well as providing the highest performance." The 1911cc DW remained in production until September 1965 when the 90bhp 1985cc engine was introduced. Thereafter, a manual version of the Slough DS was designated the DS19A.

DW development was influenced by the introduction of the Connaught GT, and ID conversion for high performance driving by Surrey Citroën dealer, Connaught Cars of Portsmouth Road, Send, a firm of repute when it came to Grand Prix racing. Connaught's director, racing driver Rodney Clarke, had seen the potential of modifying the 66bhp ID19 by fitting a DS cylinder head of the 8-port type,

raising compression from 7.5 to 8.5:1, and fitting higher rate spring valves, domed pistons, and an inlet manifold to Citroén's original design. The DS four-coil ignition system was used, a lighter flywheel fitted, and the braking and steering systems uprated so as to be fully powered: fitment of twin Solex, SU or Weber carburettors ensured rapid acceleration. Maximum speed of the Connaught GTs is somewhat academic, ranging from 97mph (156km/h) to 105mph (169km/h) depending on the level of engine tuning and which road test is consulted. Fuel consumption is also academic, but taking an average, it dropped from the ID's 26.3mpg to 23.4mpg (11lts/100km to 12lts/100km), of little consequence to the owner intent on achieving high performance motoring.

Some 200 IDs were converted by Connaught, with rubbing strips along their lower flanks in similar fashion to the yet-to-be introduced DS 21 Pallas. In place of the usual seating, the Connaught had front bucket seats, the single-spoke steering wheel giving way to a Stirling Moss-type wheel, while the dashboard mirrored that of the DS. Among the sportier circles of Citroën enthusiasts, Connaughts were revered because of their outstanding performance, and the late John Bolster gave the car credibility when he penned

The unique
CITROEN DECAPOTABLE

A mere fifty Décapotables *were officially imported into the United Kingdom. All were supplied directly from Paris, and the regulation number plate, together with other specific UK market trim items, were supplied to Chapron from the Slough factory. (Author's collection)*

a glowing report extolling its virtues to readers of *Autosport* in August 1963. Rodney Clarke, in company with others in the motor sport fraternity, appreciated only too well the merits of front-wheel drive Citroëns, the Slough-built *Traction Avant* having been the favoured mode of transport for the likes of John Heath, George Abecassis, and Sir Stirling Moss. W. O. Bentley, too, was among the Citroën's admirers and used a prewar example for company business. With the arrival of the DS and ID at Slough, Clarke could see the potential for a high performance conversion that would attract the sporting enthusiast; however, the decision to abandon assembly of vehicles at Slough brought about the demise of the Connaught GT, a very fast Citroën.

BRITISH MARKET DÉCAPOTABLES

The most expensive Citroëns in the British catalogue, *Décapotables* - marketed in the UK as Drophead Coupés - were never constructed at Slough but imported from France. Only fifty were sold to the most demanding and discriminating customers, and surviving cars are highly revered by their owners. Built by Henri Chapron at Levallois to special order, cars destined for UK customers were constructed to British specification, incorporating the regulatory number plate mountings, bumpers, lights, badging, and other components, all of which were supplied from Slough.

THE END OF CAR MANUFACTURE AT SLOUGH

The Slough-built DS and IDs were never high volume sellers, contributory factors being the cars' complexity and radical styling, along with relatively high prices. Added to this, some stigma still attached to foreign cars,

even though these cars were built in Britain by locally employed people. Slough had, for decades, supplied Commonwealth countries with right-hand drive Citroëns, an important market for the Slough factory with the *Traction Avant* having been especially successful. There is no doubt that when introduced to the United Kingdom, the DS was expected to be as popular as its predecessor. Circumstances changed dramatically as far as British production was concerned when South Africa, closely followed by Australia, opened Citroën manufacturing bases of their own, receiving components direct from Paris for assembly rather than buying complete cars from Slough.

Manufacturing technology and marketing trends were also changing, indicating that a limited assembly facility, like that at Slough, was no longer economically viable. During the 1960s, therefore, production at Slough declined drastically, casting doubt on the future of the British operation. In an effort to offset Slough's rising overheads and manufacturing costs, and help streamline French production,

a policy change called for drastic assembly changes from September 1964. Instead of all vehicles being assembled from CKD parts, they would arrive from France in a semi-assembled condition (SKD) with all mechanical and hydraulic components *in situ*. Slough's operation was therefore reduced to installing the electrics, trimming the interiors, and doing final painting and testing. This measure was intended as a stopgap only; a dramatic review of operations at Slough was inevitable. For any car factory 8668 vehicles (DS and ID) produced over a decade is hardly economical, despite the Slough works having provided the UK with a unique and essential contribution to the country's motor industry and national economy over a period of forty years. The decision was taken to close the Slough manufacturing facility from 18th February 1966, forty years to the day after its grand opening by none other than André Citroën.

From the date the assembly lines fell silent at Slough, the works continued as a distribution depot for those right-hand drive cars imported for the UK market from Paris. The factory also served as a service centre and parts stockist, as well as Citroën's administrative offices. For Citroën customers and dealers alike, Slough was the essential point of contact, whether details of new cars were required or technical assistance sought. One telephone call or visit to the parts counter would summon immediate help and supply of the most obscure part, however vague the description.

In 1974 the Slough factory closed, and the premises were sold to Mars Confectionary. Citroën moved to new offices and workshops in Mill Street, and in more recent years relocated to Slough Estates, on the opposite side of the Bath Road to where the company was first established.

Slough DSs are a rarity. Of the 8667 Ds built at Slough, 2878 were DS models and 3857 IDs were destined for the home market. This late example was photographed at an enthusiasts' rally in the mid-1990s. (Author's collection)

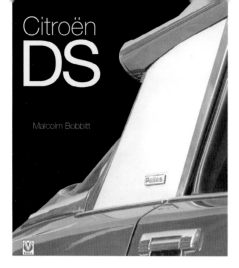

Citroën DS

Malcolm Bobbitt

CHAPTER EIGHT

NEW DIRECTIONS

These fine surroundings make a very fitting backdrop for the graceful lines of the Goddess. The overall size of the car, in this instance a DS21 Pallas, can be gauged to a large extent by its wheelbase, which is identical to that of the Rolls-Royce Silver Cloud. Within months of this photograph being taken the DS underwent serious styling modifications. (Brian Chandler collection)

In September 1967 the face of the DS was substantially modified to a bold new look that was daringly innovative. The already very-different-to-any-other-car DS, which had been in production for a little over a decade, underwent a discretionary styling transformation that made it all the more remarkable. The by now familiar lines of the Goddess were unchanged, and her spirit remained the same, but she became even more sylph-like with a new shape that was both elegant and assertive; the reshaped front wings and redesigned nose giving a definite shark-like look.

It was inevitable that the DS model range would undergo some redevelopment; Bertoni's continual styling exercises were an indication of what was to come. Just how Bertoni decided on the transformation is the subject of rumour and counter-rumour; some say that the Italian stylist went to work in his studio on the front of a car in a moment of furious inspiration, others that the styling exercises were premeditated.

Flaminio Bertoni died more than three years before the revised DS range of cars was introduced at the Paris Salon in the autumn of 1967. His successor, Robert Opron, has on various occasions provided some illuminating background to Bertoni's career. Opron suggests that Bertoni was at odds with

Before his untimely death in February 1964 Flaminio Bertoni had undertaken styling exercises to reshape the nose of the DS. The transformation was completed by Bertoni's successor, Robert Opron, and this cut-away model of the DS suitably displays modifications that remained largely unchanged until production ceased. (Courtesy Citroën)

the design of the DS, which the Italian claimed once to have been inspired by the outline of a fish. Full appreciation of Bertoni's skill came when a wheelless DS, looking rather like a spaceship in flight, was famously exhibited at the Milan Triennale in October 1957. That image is now quite familiar, and

*In September 1966 the DS's hydraulic system was extensively modified, LHM (*Liquide Hydraulique Minérale*) replacing the corrosive and hygroscopic castor-oil based and synthetic fluids (LHS). This Citroën publicity document graphically illustrates the workings of the DS's lifeblood. (Courtesy Citroën)*

has been used throughout Citroën's publicity material as an example of the car's futuristic design.

Robert Opron had been involved in the DS's restyling process since the early 1960s when a number of styling themes were produced, some of which reflect the *Bureau d'Etudes'* thinking about the future and the models proposed. Common to these ideas is a radical lighting arrangement calling for a re-working of the front wings. Before getting too deeply involved in the new-look Goddess, it's pertinent to review the car's technical developments during the mid-1960s, a hectic period in the life of the DS which immediately preceded changes designed to take effect for the 1968 model year. Engine specifications for both the DS and ID came under scrutiny and were uprated, the original 1911cc units being reliable and long-lived, though somewhat unrefined: agricultural was the term used most often. Introduced in September 1965, the 90bhp 1985cc unit was fitted to the DS19A, while the 109bhp engine, from October the same year, powered the DS21. For the ID range of cars the faithful 1911cc continued in various outputs until September 1966 - after which the 84bhp 1985cc unit continued for two years until September 1968.

1966 was a watershed in DS technology. The new engines - now with five-bearing crankshafts but continuing as developments of the unit that had evolved throughout the *Traction* era - were mated to a new gearbox, producing livelier performance. This increased power and smoother operation overall was welcomed by customers.

At the same time as the new engines arrived, both DS and ID cars were treated to modified suspension and transmission technology, courtesy of redesigned front suspension arms and tripod CV joints at the transmission end of the driveshafts. The braking system was also revised to use twin-caliper front brakes. The unusual type of wheels, with their centre-stud fixings, were replaced by those with 5-stud fixings, and Michelin's new high performance XAS-asymmetric tyres were specified. Another change was the adoption of self-adjusting (not to be confused with swivelling) headlamps for the DS21, which meant that when braking or accelerating, which would normally cause the beams to deflect, they remained at the desired angle. The changes were confined to top-of-the-range models so ID customers were denied this technology, for the time being at any rate.

Changes and modifications to the DS and ID models made them more similar and what differences still existed were nominal, and are covered elsewhere in this chapter. Because of this trend, the ID was no longer considered an economy variant of the DS.

A landmark modification in the history of the DS and its siblings concerned that of the car's hydropneumatics when, from September 1966, the hydraulic system received a complete transfusion. The matter of hydraulic fluid had occupied Citroën's design and engineering departments long before introduction of the 15 Six H in pre-DS days. The fluids originally adopted, and those specified from 1964, were problematic inasmuch as they were hygroscopic, so called for relatively high maintenance of the hydraulic system. The fluids, coloured red, attracted moisture and would corrode system components, corrosion being most prevalent in cases of poor maintenance or if vehicles had been left idle for months at a time. A nightmare scenario was finding red fluid leaking from beneath a car but, during the DS's formative years, this was far from uncommon, and gave this unconventional car its reputation for being eccentric at best and unreliable, unpredictable and temperamental at worst.

By changing to a mineral-based fluid known as LHM (*Liquide Hydraulique Minérale*) Citroën's hydropneumatics became completely reliable. LHM was user-friendly and less reliant on regular maintenance, as was castor oil-based and synthetic LHS fluids. One major problem did still exist, though: LHM was not compatible with either of these fluids and accidentally mixing them was a recipe for disaster. Contaminating an LHM system with LHS meant that the car's entire hydraulic system had to be drained and cleaned, which was both costly and time-consuming. To prevent contamination, LHM fluid cars had hydraulic components and reservoirs painted green, whereas cars using the earlier fluid had these painted black. Handling LHM was also a lot cleaner than the other fluids, and spillage on a car's paintwork did not result

Hydraulic Circuit Diagram

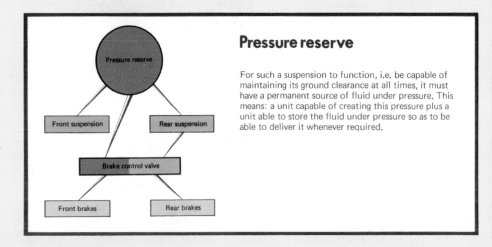

Hydraulic Gear Selector
Front Suspension Unit
3-way Union
High Pressure Pump
Front Brake Unit

Front Brake Accumulator
Pressure Regulator
Connection to Power Steering
Front Height Corrector

Feed to Rear Brake Valve
Brake Pedal Gear Union Flange
Feed to Brake Pressure Distributor
Pressure Warning Switch
Priority Valve
Feed to Front Brake Valve

Rear Brake
Rear Suspension Cylinder
Rear Height Corrector

High Pressure

Feed to Height Correctors

Suspension

Brakes

Principle: a pump operated by the engine draws a special fluid from a tank (or reservoir) and delivers it to a pressure accumulator via a pressure regulator. This pressure regulator imposes a limit on the pressure of the fluid pumped into the accumulator when maximum pressure has been reached in the latter. The regulator also allows fluid delivered by the pump to be returned to the reservoir (easily and at very low pressure) thus relieving the pump. From the pressure accumulator the fluid under pressure is routed to the various hydraulic units it serves.

Pressure reserve

Front suspension · Rear suspension

Brake control valve

Front brakes · Rear brakes

Pressure reserve

For such a suspension to function, i.e. be capable of maintaining its ground clearance at all times, it must have a permanent source of fluid under pressure. This means: a unit capable of creating this pressure plus a unit able to store the fluid under pressure so as to be able to deliver it whenever required.

Styling modifications are shown to good effect on this manual transmission DS21 owned by Alf Turner and pictured in France. In recent years the owner has swopped the car's DS21 engine for a fuel-injected DS23 unit which gives outstanding performance. (Courtesy Brian Drummond)

This is the face of the DS that most people recognise. The bold new look has timeless styling. (Courtesy Brian Drummond)

Right: The modified headlamp arrangement of this DS Pallas *can be seen in good detail, the inner long range lamps being designed to swivel in accordance with the steering mechanism. Whilst standard on the* Pallas, *swivelling headlamps were optional on other models. The rectangular vents in the front bumper indicate that this car has air conditioning. (Courtesy Brian Drummond)*

self-adjusting outer units as previously. The inner lamps provided long-range illumination, a feature greeted enthusiastically by DS owners who had become resigned to poor nighttime visibility. What made this headlamp pattern so unique was that on *Pallas* models the inner driving lamps cleverly swivelled to follow the direction of steering, giving rise to all sorts of claims, one of the more memorable (and completely false) being that here was

in it blistering or being permanently damaged; nor did containers corrode and leak, which made storage much safer.

COMPLETING THE TRANSFORMATION

From a visual aspect the most dramatic change to the D-Series cars was a new frontal mien. Not only were the bumpers redesigned, with a modified, slimmer air intake, but the direction indicators were longer to match the new profile. Front wings were redesigned to incorporate a radical and innovative headlamp arrangement: encased beneath glass visors that conformed to the leading shape of each wing were twin headlamps, with

The new look of the DS in detail. Along with twin faired-in headlamps under glass covers, there are new direction indicators, air intake and bumpers. The stripes on the glass headlamp covers are there for no purpose other than decoration. (Courtesy Brian Drummond)

'72 CITROËN ⌃

Above: DSs specified for the American market were denied swivelling headlamps and glass covers because of local legislation. Note the round direction indicators fitted to the valence as required for USA market cars, also the air conditioning vents. In the background can be seen a Citroën 5CV, popular in the UK during the early 1920s. (Courtesy Dave Shepherd)

Left: This publicity brochure illustration clearly shows the modifications necessary in order to export cars to America. Federal Safety Standards (FSS) insisted that it should be possible for replacement sealed beam headlamps, available at drug stores, to be fitted with just a simple screwdriver. (Brian Chandler collection)

DS 21 Pallas   **DS 21**   **D Special**

a car which could see around corners! A standard feature of *Pallas* models, therefore, swivelling headlamps could be specified on DS models, and for most customers they were essential. The new frontal design was adopted across the range of DS and ID models at the same time. When the swivelling headlamp option was not specified, the car's inner lamps remained fixed, as they were on those models without power-assisted steering.

Throughout the career of the DS, changes to specification according to year and model designation were always convoluted, and even now, some thirty years since the last car left the production line, inconsistencies are being discovered. One particular irregularity concerned that of UK market vehicles which received swivelling headlamps on all DS models, whether or not they were built to *Pallas* specification. Non-DS models, - successor to the ID - were not given directional headlamps unless specified as an option.

Cars specified for the American market were not only denied swivelling headlamps, but it was actually illegal to have the glass cowlings fitted, the reason being that America's Federal Safety Standards (known as FSS) demanded that sealed beam headlamps be fitted, replacements for which could be purchased at any drug store and fitted to the car with no greater mechanical expertise than knowing how to use a screwdriver! DS models exported to the USA were therefore modified to meet FSS regulations and arguably lost some of their appeal

in the process. Another US market requirement was (on pre-1968 model year cars) provision of round pod-like front direction indicators to replace the flush-fitting rectangular type. Post 1968 DSs destined for America were fitted with circular indicators on under-bumper valances; indicators beneath the headlamps were blanked off although amber side reflectors were fitted to the front wings. The rear lighting on American market cars was similar to that of British cars: round Lucas lamps and indicator lenses.

There were several more US-specific requirements. Emission controls were enforced from 1968, which meant that, from that date, all DSs were required to conform to stringent regulations. Closed crankcase ventilation and catalytic converters (on late model cars) were necessary, and facia panels had to have rocker-type switches. Air conditioning was favoured and headrests fitted as standard from 1969. Emission control regulations differed throughout the USA according to the state, with the most stringent being California. Ultimately it became too costly to export cars to the USA where the number of Citroën agents had declined to nearly a third of what they had been at the start of DS exports; sales to the US were withdrawn in 1972.

The DS's swivelling headlamp technology was as controversial as its hydraulic wizardry. A parking manoeuvre in a crowded road guaranteed an audience, fascinated by the swivelling headlamps. Add to that, of course, the audible clicking

of the vehicle's hydraulic pump, and the hissing sound as the LHM entered and drained from its reservoir, and there was no doubt that the car was a Citroën.

The swivelling headlamps were operated via a complicated system of levers, rods and cables which connected to the car's steering rack. As the steering wheel was turned, so the driving lamps would activate, their angle of movement slightly exaggerated to compensate for the outward stance of the car's cornering geometry. This slight exaggeration also gave a wider beam of light. Where the arrangement really came into its own, though, was along rural unlit roads, and especially at road junctions, lighting up the way ahead in advance of turning.

The powerful driving lamps with their quartz iodine bulbs (available as an option, in which case cars were fitted with a larger capacity battery to cope with the power demand) were definitely an aid to long-distance travelling. An unnerving side effect, though, was that when switching from main beam to dipped, the lights went out momentarily, plunging the road into darkness. DS owners, however, soon became accustomed to the peculiarities of the lighting system, and there was a marked improvement in performance when quartz lamps were eventually specified for use with dipped beams.

One can be forgiven for believing that swivelling headlamps are another Citroën innovation but, like the famous single-spoke steering wheel, swivelling headlamps had been tried before,

stylists were reluctant to phase in a completely new instrument panel in one fell swoop; for the next model year, 1970, the job was completed by replacing the wide rectangular instruments with three large dials, one housing the speedometer, another the rev counter, and the third incorporating

Self-adjusting headlights.

Standard on all DS models except D Special. Main beams are self-levelling—remain constantly parallel with road. Inboard headlights turn with front wheels to precede you round bends and add extra light for fast night driving. All four headlights are quartz-iodine.

Interior luxury and safety.

Inside the DS, seats are contoured, floors are carpeted, instrumentation is complete with all controls intelligently positioned. Leg, head and elbow room are generous for five people. Visibility is panoramic. Upholstery hardwearing Targa or soft, gripping Jersey nylon (optional)

albeit without a great deal of success or reliability. Possibly the most bizarre use of swivelling headlamps was promoted by Preston Thomas Tucker when he introduced his Tucker Sedan in 1948. Tucker's designs were renowned for being highly innovative; his Sedan had an enormous horizontally-opposed, 9652cc, all-aluminium engine with an output of just 150bhp. Swivelling mudguards and headlamps were part of the car's original specification but, ultimately, it was only the central

'Cyclops' lamp which swivelled with the steering.

In contrast to the striking restyling of the DS's face, the facia - with its already unconventional instrumentation - continued unchanged. It was another year before a new dashboard layout appeared, and even then the changes appeared fairly minor at first glance. Whilst instrumentation remained fairly similar to the earlier pattern, rectangular push-button switches replaced the round versions. It seems that Citroën

a comprehensive warning display. At the centre of the warning indicator display a central red 'stop' lamp glowed menacingly to alert the driver to something seriously amiss, such as loss of hydraulic pressure or overheating.

What of the new slab-shaped dashboard with its crackle-type metal finished in depressing black paint? It was hardly lovely-to-look-at compared to Bertoni's masterpiece but it was functional and had clear-to-read instruments. It was modern, too, with

Alf Turner's elegant DS21 pictured in its native France at Audierne in Bretagne. From a driver's point of view the swivelling headlamp approach gives completely efficient lighting. To enhance the DS's lighting still further, some owners have fitted halogen bulbs. Citroën's C4 model announced in 2004 is fitted with directional headlamps.
(Courtesy Brian Drummond)

1970 model year DSs were specified with an all-new facia incorporating round dials. In this photograph note that the 'old style' steering wheel is retained; later modifications meant that a new padded wheel was fitted.
(Courtesy Citroën)

an almost aggressive appearance about it, reflecting current styling trends. The majority of customers approved and, in retrospect, it has appeal.

Dashboard design revisions were made throughout the range of D-Series cars, albeit with a number of anomalies, such as the steering wheel which was modified and padded - the so-called 'safety wheel' - on the DS and *Pallas* from September 1971, but not on lesser models for another couple of years. Equipment levels were decided on a model's status and specification, so that the less expensive models didn't

Guy Pursey arriving at Madeira Drive, Brighton, when competing in the 2001 London to Brighton Classic & Sportscar Run. (Courtesy Dick Lankester)

Guy Pursey's D Super has featured in a number of television programmes and magazine articles. This splendid car is pictured here at Waddesdon Manor in England. (Courtesy Sue Magnan)

have a clock or superior trim items.

Revisions to the overall model range in 1969 included new front seats that had taller backrests for greater comfort and support. Fabric material and trim differed according to model, but a definite improvement was the reclining mechanism, a wheel tilting the backrest to the desired position rather than the knurled screw fittings which gave only two positions, fully raised or fully lowered. The styling and technological transformation of the D-Series cars was therefore complete. A revision of the model range in respect of equipment and trim specification meant that disparities between the DS and ID were significantly reduced.

THE POWER CURVE

Two new models came on-line for 1969: the DS20, with the 103bhp, 1985cc engine replacing the venerable DS19; and the 103bhp ID20. The DS21 also received more power, increasing the 2175cc engine to 115bhp from 109, whilst the ID19 remained in production but was uprated to 91bhp. Two versions of the ID19 were marketed

- Confort and Luxe - though the latter was renamed the Export in March. Compared to the Confort, the Export's specification hardly warrants a second thought, so basic was it, and within six months the model was deleted from the catalogue.

The differences between ID and DS models were reduced to the point where, for the 1970 model year, the ID20 was marketed as the D Super, and the lower powered ID19 was designated the D Spécial. In essence the D Super was promoted to the rank of DS but with manual transmission, and with it a general upgrading of trim materials: vestiges of ID furnishings remained, however, such as plastic door handles and vinyl headlining. This coincided very neatly with deletion from the catalogue of the manual version DS20, while the DS21 received Bosch fuel injection as an option.

Adoption of fuel injection raised the DS's - and Citroën's - profiles enormously. With a maximum speed of 115mph (185km/h), the DS21 was catapulted to being among the fastest vehicles in Europe. At £2223, which

was £240 more expensive than the carburettor version of the DS21, the EFI version, as it became known, was still in the Jaguar league when it came to price, and was substantially more expensive than Rover's P6 2000 series, even in its most costly configuration. (Rover engineers had examined the DS in great detail when considering the P6's design and styling principles between 1956 and 1958, and a number of DS styling cues are evident in the P6.)

The DS21 was the first mass produced car in France to be equipped with electronic fuel injection. It was also only the second car in Europe to have EFI, the first being a Mercedes. Developed by Bosch, the system incorporated a computer, installed under the instrument panel on the passenger side of the vehicle, to precisely calculate the amount of fuel required for injection. In order for the injection system to work efficiently, Citroën engineers had to completely overhaul the car's fuel system and modify the petrol tank, as well as uprate the cooling system. Having a power gain of nearly 20 per cent over the carburettor car, it was necessary

What's the collective noun for a group of Goddesses? (Courtesy Brian Drummond)

to specify larger section tyres - 185 section all round. Compared to the 13.7 seconds the DS21 normally took to reach 60mph (97km/h), the fuel-injected car took only 12.4 seconds.

Further standardisation of the model range followed in 1971. All left-hand drive cars were fitted with foot-operated parking brakes, although in right-hand drive vehicles the under-dash pendant device continued. This was because there was insufficient room to locate the pedal, and, in any case, British motorists seemed quite unreceptive to such an arrangement, as was evident with the XM: for some reason, British motorists find such a system awkward to use and co-ordinate. Five-speed gearboxes became available, giving more relaxed cruising and greater fuel economy; the exception was the D Spécial which retained the four-speed 'box.

The following year there was a 5bhp increase in power for the DS21, which could also now be had with air conditioning, not as a dealer option but factory-fitted. Air conditioning was more popular in markets outside France than the home market where it was considered an expensive and unwanted luxury. Those cars fitted with air conditioning (identified externally by four slim rectangular air intakes cut into each side of the front bumper) had a somewhat cumbersome ventilation and control unit installed below the centre of the dashboard which protruded into the cabin area. Fully automatic transmission, in the form of the Borg-Warner Type 35 system, also

became available. From a customer satisfaction viewpoint the Borg-Warner transmission - when fitted to the DS - was not a success; owners of fully automatic cars complained of excessive fuel consumption, and dissatisfaction increased when gearboxes began to fail after just moderate mileages, often not exceeding 70,000 miles.

All models built for the 1972 model year onward were fitted with recessed door handles which improved the cars' appearance no end, as well as being a safety requirement introduced by various manufacturers during the early 1970s. Power increases, as with the DS21, were carried through to the D Spécial and D Super, to 98 and 108bhp respectively.

TWO NEW MODELS

When in August 1972 the D Super 5 made its appearance, it became one of the most sought-after cars in the catalogue. Coupled with a five-speed gearbox the car was fully equipped, including power steering. It had spirited performance, too, the DS21's 2175cc engine producing 115bhp. The car was popular with British customers who appreciated its power and economy with superb comfort, and who discovered it to have directional lights as standard for the 1974 model year.

Meanwhile, changes to the D Super and D Spécial meant that these models were denied the five-speed gearbox although specification was upgraded generally, the latter model

receiving the 108bhp engine. For the British market the D Super 5 took over from the D Super which was withdrawn from the catalogue.

The fastest and most powerful version of the DS arrived in August 1972 for the 1973 model year. This was the DS23, Citroën's executive express and true successor to the fabled DS19 of 1955. Available with or without fuel-injection, and the option of manual transmission, hydraulic or fully automatic Borg-Warner gearbox, this was the ultimate Citroën. From the 2347cc engine there developed 124bhp, rising to a massive 141bhp when fuel injected to offer a whisker under 120mph (192.5km/h) maximum speed. Compared to the already luxurious D Super 5, here was total opulence. Sit back in those wonderfully soft but totally supportive armchairs: flick the gear selector and let the hydraulic transmission propel the car to previously impossible speeds; smoothly; graciously; effortlessly; without a hint of fuss …

From this angle the Goddess makes for a particularly fetching picture. The Webasto sun roof is non-standard but a number of owners opted to have it fitted. The external trim detail with brightwork along the door tops and lower flanks show this to be a Pallas model; the recessed door handles date the car as a post 1972 model. (Courtesy John White)

Two faces of the Goddess. The car on the left is a late model, and that on the right is Joe Judt's rare right-hand drive Décapotable. (Courtesy Brian Drummond)

Reviewing the DS23 *Pallas* EFI in February 1973, *Motor* was a lot less appreciative of the plush ride and positive handling, which was far superior to that of the Silver Shadow with its Citroën-supplied, self-levelling arrangement. Harsh and fussy were the words used to describe the Queen of the *Routes Nationales*, and the tester dared suggest that the suspension was equalled and even surpassed by the springing of some conventional cars. What about those brakes? Oversensitive was the claim - an argument lost when real emergency stopping was required. And when it came to lifting the bonnet the hapless driver had difficulty tracking down the dipstick, such was the extent of the plumbing in the engine bay, said the magazine. In non-*Pallas* trim the car remained available for two years only, thereafter available in *Pallas* option only. Lucky were those who visited their Citroën showroom to order this beautiful beast when they had the chance ...

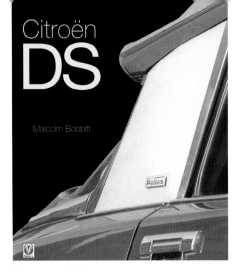

Citroën DS

Malcolm Bobbitt

CHAPTER NINE

END OF AN ERA

A Goddess is at home anywhere!
(Courtesy Tony Stokoe/Brian
Scott-Quinn)

For a car to remain in production for two decades is remarkable, and only the most outstanding - the Volkswagen Beetle, Morris Minor, Fiat 500 and, of course, Citroën's *Traction Avant* - have achieved this longevity. It's even more unusual for a design to appear as novel and exciting twenty years after it first appeared, yet this is the case with the DS.

The DS's arrival in 1955 was opportune. Post war austerity was being replaced with growing prosperity, and the *avant-garde* Citroën seemed to epitomise this sea change. The *Traction Avant* had been instrumental in changing the course of automobile design but, by the mid-1950s, though still technically advanced compared to many other cars, it was seriously outdated. The Goddess took up where the *Traction Avant* left off and carried innovation and technology to new and exciting limits, the pinnacle of Citroën achievement. No model since has taken such a big leap forward in technology, nor made such an unequivocal statement.

Citroën's big problem before introduction of the highly innovative GS in the early 1970s was that it had nothing to offer by way of a mid-range car, a market sector that other vehicle manufacturers found particularly lucrative but one which Citroën had ignored. With the 425cc 2CV ably accompanied from 1961 by the 602cc *Ami* 6 at one end, and the D-Series at the other, there was a huge gap in the catalogue. It was left to Renault, Peugeot and Simca to satisfy the market and profit from it. Panhard

was also within the same market sector, until, that is, it was acquired by Citroën which, unhappily, let it fall into obscurity.

Citroën would have you believe that the *Ami* 6 was in fact within the medium car market. Fundamentally a re-clothed 2CV with an air-cooled flat-twin engine enlarged to 602cc, it was, nevertheless, more accommodating than the *Deux Chevaux*, and in estate car form carried a relatively large payload. Nevertheless, the *Ami* was fairly and squarely categorised as a small car.

A number of proposals for a mid-range car were evaluated, and one in particular almost reached production. This was Flaminio Bertoni's C60, a machine totally eccentric in the Citroën sense with styling cues taken from the DS, and others that were to be incorporated on the yet-to-be-announced *Ami* 6. Evident on the C60, which was proposed during the late 1950s and early '60s and abandoned in favour of the Ami 6, was a glimpse of the DS's post 1968 headlamp configuration as well as the reverse rake rear window as seen on the *Ami* and Ford Anglia. Flaminio Bertoni's styling for the C60 was predictably dramatic: add to this hydropneumatic suspension and a flat-four air-cooled

engine and the beginnings of what was to become the GS concept can be recognised. However, immediately before the C60 was due to be signed off for production, Citroën management decided it was too unconventional, even by its standards. Whether the C60 would have worked well in Citroën's favour is debatable; French motorists had, after all, come to expect something quirky from the company.

With Citroën's A-series model making a substantial profit, the D-Series was less successful in this area. Pierre Bercot, when reviewing Citroën's fortunes during the DS era, was moved to admit that the Goddess was perceived by many as an extravagance the company could ill afford. No other manufacture, apart from a handful of specialist luxury car makers, could afford to build a vehicle to the same engineering quality as the DS. While certainly not an indulgence on Citroën's part, the DS was an expensive car to construct, at least according to Citroën's bean counters. Because of the car's engineering complexity, many potential customers, worried about maintenance and reliability, chose instead models which, although maybe less attractive and without the DS's individuality, were rather more straightforward.

For the DS to have been completely profitable, production output of in excess of 500 cars a day would have been necessary, in Bercot's estimation.

That it never reached this figure says much about the company's finances. Taking DS production as a whole throughout the twenty years from 1955, the daily average of cars leaving Citroën assembly lines is less than 300, rising to around 400 during the peak years of 1960 through to 1973.

When the new-look DS was being launched in 1968, Michelin, successor to the original Citroën company, was considering the future of its vehicle manufacturing enterprise. The global motor industry was already undergoing change via a process of co-operation and amalgamation, which included the French. In 1963 a limited agreement had been reached between Peugeot and Citroën with regard to material purchase, and three years later Renault and Peugeot signed an agreement to build Renault's 8 and 10 models alongside the Peugeot 404 at the Saint-Bruno factory near Montréal.

In 1968 Peugeot and Renault further combined activities to build a factory at Douvrin-la-Bassée in northern France to construct engines common to both manufacturers. Volvo joined the two French car makers in the engine enterprise under the name 'France Swedish PRV Engines' whose manufacturing facility was known as Société Française de Mécanique, a joint Peugeot-Renault venture established with a 50 million franc capital. The arrangement between Peugeot and Citroën continued and a 'Douvrin' 2-

litre engine eventually found its way under the bonnet of the Citroën CX, in 1979.

Thus it made sense, to Michelin management at least, that to combine efforts with a suitable partner might be the most profitable route to take. After a number of unsuccessful negotiations an arrangement with Fiat was established in 1968, but this did not endure beyond 1973. On learning of a possible agreement with Fiat, Peugeot and Renault made a joint approach to Citroën to join the partnership, which, if it had materialised, would have had the backing of the French government. Michelin, however, was having nothing to do with it.

During the five year period in which there was collaboration with Fiat, Citroën took two bold steps: unveiling at Geneva in March 1970 its super sports coupé, the SM, a product of a marriage between Maserati and Citroën, more of which later; and introducing the mid-size GS at the Paris Salon in October 1970. Both projects were a severe drain on Citroën's resources, and compounding the issue was ongoing work on development of an eventual successor to the DS, which also required significant investment. Add to this the massive injection of funds necessary to build a new factory at Aulnay-sous-Bois on the outskirts of Paris, and it is obvious that Citroën was a powerful drain on Michelin resources.

In Michelin's negotiations with

The new-look DS was launched in 1968, by which time Michelin, successor to the company founded by André Citroën, was deliberating whether or not to sell off its motor manufacturing business. (Author's collection)

Europe's car makers it had even been suggested that Citroën should be sold to the highest bidder. That the Double Chevron emblem might fall into obscurity was unthinkable, though such a possibility had existed even before Michelin's acquisition of the firm.

During the early months of 1974 the price of oil dramatically escalated, rising by a factor of four. Immediately prior to the oil crisis, during the autumn of 1973, vehicle sales throughout Europe nose dived: a drop of 44 per cent was recorded in Germany; in the Netherlands 40 per cent, and in Belgium 34 per cent. Elsewhere sales drop-offs were slightly lower with the United Kingdom and Italy both recording 21

per cent. France escaped with just nine per cent. For Michelin, vehicle and tyre supplier throughout Europe and beyond, the knock-on effect was drastic: in order to offset huge losses the decision was made to sell Citroën.

Control of Citroën transferred from Michelin to Peugeot in July

Michelin accepted that Citroën was a very marketable company with a prestigious name. Citroëns were favoured by services and organisations throughout Europe, including the French Gendarmerie. (Author's collection)

DSs operated by the Gendarmerie Nationale *were once a familiar sight on roads throughout France.*
(Author's collection)

1974, but it was not until 1976 that the merger of the two companies was ratified. Peugeot acquired nearly 90 per cent (89.95 per cent, to be precise) of Citroën's capital and Peugeot Limited became PSA Peugeot Citroën. For Citroën this initially proved an unhappy state of affairs: Peugeot and Citroën were worlds apart when it came to design and innovation - Citroën the adventurous motivator was stymied by Peugeot's prudence, and Peugeot management quickly ousted any Citroën staff who persisted in pursuing radical engineering ideas. Peugeot confined the *Bureau d'Etudes* to levels of activity that could do little harm to the company's reputation for producing excellent cars which, nevertheless, were of conservative design. In Peugeot's eyes the DS was politically incorrect, and Citroën models in general too technically advanced and peculiar for their own good. Such technology, Peugeot argued, could easily prove a sales deterrent and therefore financially disastrous. Not surprisingly, therefore, one of the first

casualties of the Peugeot takeover was Robert Opron.

Peugeot recognised that Citroën customers wanted much more from their cars than conformist styling and conventional engineering. There would, for the foreseeable future, be room for Citroën's *avant-garde* policies, even if these were watered down somewhat; in the short term the future for the DS, looked very bleak indeed.

At the time of Peugeot's acquisition of Citroën, the DS was one of the most individual and technically advanced cars in the world. Quite simply, the DS was not Peugeot's type of car, even though it was the choice of the establishment, government ministers - and even the French President!

FINAL YEARS OF THE DS

Development of the D-Series range, as we have seen, called for an overall convergence of models so that, in reality, the D Spécial and D Super were far more akin to the DS than had been the case with the ID. Levels of trim and the materials used for the D Spécial and D Super were far superior to those employed on earlier cars, to the extent that a cursory glance wasn't always sufficient to distinguish them from more expensive variants. There

were tell-tale signs, of course: rubbing strips were applied to the Pallas and Prestige; rear quarter panels were fluted, and D Spécials and Supers were fitted with smaller hubcaps, although export models (including RHD vehicles) received the larger type. From September 1965 identification was made easier in the respect that badging appeared on the boot lid of DS models, in various styles and with different graphics according to model and build year. ID, D Spécial, and D Super models were similarly badged, but not until September 1968.

With adoption of a universal facia, identification of later cars became less obvious, especially vehicles with manual transmission. Neither hydraulic gear selection nor the Borg-Warner fully automatic gearbox was ever fitted to any of the ID models or their successors, and all left-hand drive IDs received the pendant-type brake pedal, the brakes conforming to ID circuitry rather than that of the DS. Right-hand drive models differed so that the D Super and D Super 5 were more DS-like by virtue of the mushroom-operated brake pedal.

By the early 1970s the D-Series cars had been reduced to a modest level with a range of options that were

continued page 138

Below & right: The DS was so technically advanced that it could maintain momentum at speed on three wheels. The look on the motorcyclist's face says it all! (John Reynolds collection)

AJ 28.733

The rubbing strips along the lower flanks of the doors, the bright trim along the door tops at waist level, and the aluminium sill covers identify this car as a pre-1972 DS Pallas. Note the non-flush door handles. (Courtesy Tony Stokoe/Brian Scott-Quinn)

Citroën

Left: Throughout production of the D-Series models there was a convergence of specification which meant that, toward the end of their eras, the DS and ID were virtually indistinguishable from a distance. This is a D Spécial, which in left-hand drive form would have had smaller wheel trims. D Spécials and Supers were fitted with manual transmission and outsold the DS, which had more elaborate interior trim. (Courtesy Guy Pursey)

Bottom left: The design of wheel trim identifies this elegant machine as a DS23 Pallas pictured here amidst exquisite surroundings. Pallas models could be specified with manual or semi-automatic transmission. (Courtesy Tony Stokoe/Brian Scott-Quinn)

This is Shaun Lilley's superb 1973 DS 23 fuel-injected Pallas, one of the most desirable DS models, and the final DS model type to be introduced. (Courtesy Tony Stokoe/Brian Scott-Quinn)

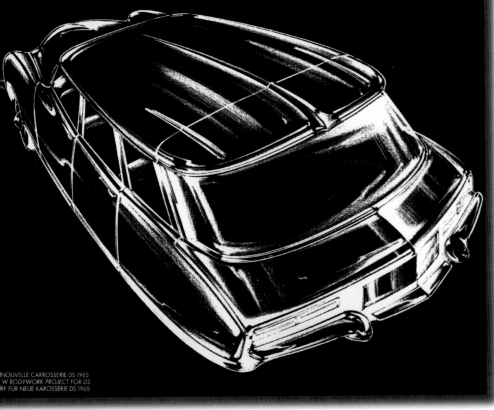

NOUVELLE CARROSSERIE DS 1965
W BODYWORK PROJECT FOR DS
RF FUR NEUE KAROSSERIE DS 1965

acceptable to as wide a market as possible. The less expensive D Spécials and Supers (in common with the ID) outsold the luxury DS models, which is one of the reasons why the series as a whole was not as profitable as it might otherwise have been. Luxurious as they were compared to other cars, Spécials and Supers lacked the sophistication of their top-of-the-range siblings. Finishing touches and attention to detail, such as rear compartment lighting so tastefully concealed at the top of C-pillars, deep-pile carpeting and the option of finest hide upholstery on *Pallas* and *Prestige* variants, are hallmarks of the DS. Incidentally, no other car maker invested so much research in car seating as Citroën, and it is doubtful whether the DS's seats could ever be surpassed for comfort and support.

Similar model convergence was applied to ID estate cars which, from August 1973, were marketed as DS Breaks. The ID nomenclature had been dropped as early as September 1969, the models being catalogued as Break 20 or 21 according to engine size. *Familiales* and *Commerciales* were similarly marketed, the latter having

been withdrawn from sale in August 1973. If the DS23 road test written for *Motor* had criticised the car for its ancient feel and performance, John Bolster's *Autosport* road test of the DS23 Safari showed the car in a totally different light. Bolster, a self-confessed admirer of the DS, appreciated the car's untiring performance over long journeys whilst maintaining high average speeds with acceptable fuel economy. The Safari's 2.3 litre engine was more refined and flexible than

previous models, maximum torque at 3500rpm affording almost effortless high speed cruising and a top speed of in excess of 100mph, even with full payloads.

DS production - including all D-Series vehicles - remained relatively stable: output steadily increased to a high point of 83,205 in 1960, thereafter averaging 90,000 per annum to the end of the 1973 model year, peaking in 1967 and 1970 with 101,904 and 103,633 units respectively. From 96,990 vehicles in 1973, production dramatically dropped to 40,039 in 1974, partly as a result of the oil crisis and partly because Citroën had introduced the CX to replace the DS. Production for 1975, the year the DS was withdrawn from the catalogue, fell to just 847 vehicles.

Incorporated in the foregoing figures, production of ID and DS Breaks also remained steady, averaging 6000

Apart from its frontal styling the new-look estate car changed little in appearance from earlier models. Pictured during a Lake District winter, this Safari is seen at Ullswater. (Courtesy Dave Ashworth/David Archer)

This could be the interior of a Citroën dealer's showroom during the early to mid-1970s. In fact, the date is much later, the late 1990s, the occasion the filming of a sequence for television about the history of the DS. (Courtesy Guy Pursey)

The DS was the first car to be built at Citroën's new factory at Aulnay-sous-Bois on the outskirts of Paris. The date is Monday 16th April 1973, and the first car, painted Ivory, leaves the production line. Part of the Aulnay factory is now home to the Citroën museum, opened in 2002/3. (Courtesy Citroën)

Successor to the DS was the CX, seen here as a series 2 variant.
(Author's collection)

On 24th April 1975 the last DS rolled off the production line at Aulnay, the 1,330,755th built in France.
(Courtesy Citroën)

vehicles a year. Unlike saloon output, which dived in 1974, that of Breaks was hardly affected, dropping 820 units from the previous year's figure of 6907. In the final year of production 75 vehicles were built.

DS PRODUCTION MOVES TO AULNAY-SOUS-BOIS

A landmark in DS production was reached on 7th October 1969 when the millionth car left the Javel production line. The factory was by then already overstretched and lacked the capacity required to build the company's entire range of vehicles. A policy of establishing factories outside Paris had been implemented early in the post war era, with the acquisition of the Automobiles Laffly works at Asnières. (This policy should not be confused with Citroën's activities in other countries where assembly plants had been

opened during the firm's formative years.) It was at Asnières that Citroën based its 'hydropneumatic facility': a new factory - the most modern in the world - was opened in 1954 where the most accurate engineering technology existed. From 1954, therefore, Asnières produced all of Citroën's hydropneumatic components under the most stringent environmental conditions.

During the early 1950s work began on the construction of a new factory in Bretagne. Known as Rennes-la-Barre-Thomas, the works opened in 1953 to supply much of Citroën's engineering components. Seven years later work began on building a new vehicle assembly plant at Rennes-la-Jannais where, initially, the 2CV, and later the Dyane, were built. With further vehicle manufacturing facilities necessary, in 1972 Citroën contracted the building of a purpose-built factory 10 miles (16km) north of Paris at Aulnay-sous-Bois, where Javel production would ultimately transfer. Within two years the factory was operational, the DS being the first car built there.

The Aulnay-sous-Bois factory was designed by Citroën-Industrie, a

division within Citroën responsible for the company's engineering operations. The works comprised four functional areas: body assembly shop, paint shop with its high-tec ovens, vehicle assembly shop, and upholstery shop, all of which used the latest technology. Citroën was no stranger to automation and procedures requiring absolute accuracy were carried out robotically. Aulnay-sous-Bois's 434 acre site (180ha) was serviced by Citroën's other factories: gearboxes from Metz; engines from Nanterre and Levallois; transmission systems from Mulhouse; hydraulics from Asnières, and other components from Froncles, Caen, and Rennes-la-Barre-Thomas.

It was on Monday 16th April 1973 that the first DS rolled off the Aulnay-sous-Bois assembly line. An auspicious occasion, the factory workforce posed alongside the car which was painted Ivoire Borely and bedecked in ribbons. A little over two years later, on 24th April 1975, the last DS, the 1,330,755th built in France, left the factory. This, too, was an auspicious occasion, even an historic one, as it signalled the end of an era.

Citroën DS

Malcolm Bobbitt

CHAPTER TEN

WITHOUT RIVAL?

It could be said that the Goddess was without a real rival. Certainly, few cars - especially in the mid-1950s - boasted such advanced technology, and neither could they match the DS's presence: a rear-view mirror sighting of a DS bearing down on you at speed is indeed awesome!

Mention has already been made of Citroën's contemporaries: in France, cars made by Renault, Peugeot, and Simca; in Britain, Jaguar, Daimler, Humber, Riley, Rover, Wolseley, and some of the more specialist marques such as Armstrong Siddeley; in Italy, Alfa Romeo's *Giulietta*, Fiat's 1900, and Lancia's *Appia* and *Aurelia*, and in Germany, the BMW 501. All or some of the cars from these manufacturers might rival the DS in terms of price and/ or performance, still others in trimming and appointment - but none in terms of technology.

It has to be said that the DS was

As a Grande Routière *or an efficient tourer the DS had few rivals, and gave a new concept to towing caravans, as its suspension was virtually impervious to the weight of the trailer. For caravan and boating enthusiasts, therefore, the Goddess was an ideal choice of vehicle.* (Brian Chandler collection)

In Britain the DS and its ID sibling had the same price tag as a Jaguar. For some it was simply no contest, though others wanted the status of a Jaguar. (Author's collection)

not everyone's choice and, for the same amount of cash, it was possible to buy a Jaguar, which might be more socially acceptable than a controversially styled foreign car. That's not to say that the DS was in any way downmarket; both cars appealed to a particular clientele who wanted to be seen driving the latest fashion accessory. The DS was the choice of the more adventurous motorist, particularly favoured by the showbiz fraternity - but what of the more conservative, traditionalist driver, to whom the thought of buying a foreign car during the fifties and sixties was abhorrent? New technology might have looked good on paper but was untried in practice, and the DS was potentially a plumber's nightmare. For many customers the decision was already made, it had to be a reputable

British sports saloon with an enviable track record and the very epitome of good taste with its wooden dashboard and finest leather upholstery, all in the best tradition.

On price alone the DS was no threat to such delectable motor cars as those made by Alvis, Bristol, and Jensen. Nor could it compete with the undoubted status of John Blatchley's finest in the shape of the S-type Bentley which made its debut at the same time. But when it comes to comfort, cabin space and handling characteristics, it's a different matter altogether: here, the DS equals (and arguably surpasses) the Bentley with its massive separate chassis, dependence on hydro-mechanical braking, and, at times, vague steering that is not helped by cross ply tyres.

Outside France, Sweden's

aerodynamic Saab 92, created by Sixten Sason and Gunnar Ljungströmand, and unveiled to the press in June 1947, possessed almost unbelievable styling. In time Saab's reputation was boosted by the marque's rallying prowess, and what the 92 lacked in engine capacity from its two-cylinder engine it made up for with sheer performance and agility. When larger engines came along, including the venerable V4, Saab built on its reputation for durability.

WOULD-BE CHALLENGERS

The fact that the DS and ID found no shortage of customers throughout Europe says much about the opposition. Like Simca, Renault offered a European-assembled American car, but failed miserably with it. The Renault Rambler was the product of an unhappy liaison with American Motors Corporation (AMC): built in Belgium from CKD kits, the operation was far from satisfactory with fewer than five thousand cars sold in five years.

The *Frégate* failed to capture the

The DS and John Blatchley's Bentley S-Type masterpiece shared identical wheelbase dimensions. Superb and refined as the Bentley is, the ride quality of the DS is superior. At one time consideration was given to fitting Citroén's self-levelling system to complement the S-Type's otherwise conventional suspension. Ultimately, it was the S-Type's successor, the Bentley T, that used Citroén technology to supplement the springing.
(Author's collection)

Saab's 92 was influenced by aircraft technology and presented superb aerodynamic styling.
(Author's collection)

Simca's Vedette featured styling that was American influenced.
(Author's collection)

Renault's Frégate, *seen here in Manoir Station Wagon guise, was no competition for the DS. Author's collection)*

Simca's Vedette *seen in good company. Note the partly hidden DS on the right and the* Traction Avant *behind. In estate car form the* Vedette *was marketed as the Marley. (Author's collection)*

imagination of French motorists and was beset by problems from the start. The design team was adamant that the car - with front engine and rear drive - should have a flat floor, just like Citroën's *Traction Avant*. The mix was disastrous: seven universal joints in the drivetrain, and an engine based on the design of that used for the 4CV but enlarged from 747cc to two litres. Performance was unimpressive and only the *Transfluide* (from 1959) with its torque converter transmission showed any potential. *Transfluide* estate cars were well appointed, and intended as direct competition to Simca's Marley, but were no match for Citroën's ID Breaks. By the early sixties it was all too late; the *Frégate* was outdated and Renault had nothing to offer in the big car league. Only when the award-winning front-wheel drive R16 arrived in 1965 did Renault have something tangible with which to rival the DS.

When Citroën introduced the *Traction Avant* in 1934, Peugeot went on the offensive with a campaign intended to discredit front-wheel drive. Twenty years later the Sochaux firm admitted to its benefits when it introduced the front-wheel drive, transverse-engined 204. Meanwhile, the 203, built from 1948 to 1960, and the 403 which arrived in 1955, were tough and willing workhorses. Those French motorists not won over by Citroën's dedication to front-wheel drive were well served by Peugeot's offerings, and for those who had a *penchant* for open top motoring, what better way to do this than in a 403 cabriolet?

Proof of the 403's rugged engineering is the fact that plentiful numbers were exported to countries where tarmac roads were unknown. Having an ability to endure much when it came to overloading and lack of maintenance, these machines serve today in environmentally hostile conditions. The 403's successor, the 404, was also destined for hard work. Available with diesel engines, 404s

Peugeot built the 203 between 1948 and 1960; it had distinctive American influences. (Author's collection)

French motorists unsure about Citroën's technology sought familiarity in the Peugeot 203. (Author's collection)

A rival to the DS came in the form of a Panhard, the 24CT pictured here. Note the headlamp design, which, it is claimed, influenced DS styling modifications. (Author's collection)

were also marketed as capacious estate cars, the family models having three rows of seats. From 1968 Peugeot's 504 sported handsome lines and more than adequate accommodation; the coupé, from 1970, featured fuel-injection and a top speed of 105mph (169km/h), whilst vehicles built from 1974 were fitted with Douvrin V6 engines.

Panhards were rivals to the DS until Citroën acquired the marque in 1965. The PL17 - despite a twin-cylinder engine - was no slouch, and demonstrated controversial styling. In *Tigre* form the PL17 produced 60bhp and top speed above that of the ID19, but it was the 24, Panhard's final offering, which was the most striking with its four-headlamp system (said to have inspired styling later applied to the DS), and svelte shape designed by Louis Bionier. In CT form (T for *Tigre*), the 24 boasted performance that was in the 100mph (160km/h) category. Had Citroën not cast Panhard into obscurity there's no knowing how the marque would have turned out.

CHALLENGE FROM BRITAIN

British rivals to the DS came from two rather unlikely sources: Rover and BMC, with the controversial P6 2000 from Rover, and the 1800 and 2200 models from BMC. Despite the fact that, in concept, the P6 2000 was similar to the pioneering DS, its conservative customers would never have contemplated buying a foreign car, and especially not one as unconventional as the Goddess.

Successor to the majestic P4 range of cars, which included the 75, 90, and

110 (forever known as Auntie Rovers), the Rover 2000 was influenced more by the DS19 than any other car. With an engineering team comprising Peter Wilks and Spen King, both of whom had had much to do with Rover's gas-turbine project, and JET 1 in particular, the incredible car which topped 150mph (241km/h) in 1952, there was no question of the new Rover being anything but sensational. Add to the mix David Bache's styling expertise and it's easy to see how the 2000 took the motor industry by storm. Here was a car that placed Rover and Britain in the forefront of automotive design, nothing quite like it had been seen before - or had it ...?

Early proposals for the 2000 had included hydropneumatic suspension, and Rover acquired a DS19 in 1958 to establish exactly how it worked. Rover's styling team had been working hard to arrive at a design that went beyond then current thinking elsewhere in the British motor industry, and what emerged was a shape that was quite innovative. Original styling concepts had included a drooping bonnet with headlamps mounted within faired pod-like housings and protruding side lights, features ultimately abandoned. While forsaking hydropneumatic suspension in favour of steel springs, Rover engineers did decide on a base

unit chassis of a stressed steel skeleton, comprising the central passenger section, inner panels separating engine compartment and boot, windscreen and door pillars, and rear quarters. Onto the base were attached mechanical components, while unstressed body panels could be hung in similar fashion to that of the DS.

The Rover design team had come to appreciate the virtues of having a rigid base platform which, ideally, was free from the effects of corrosion and allowed easy renewal of body panels in the event of accident or general deterioration. However, they discovered that while the car wore appreciably better than a monocoque design, the chassis skeleton was not as resilient to fatigue and rusting as had been anticipated. Rover made no secret of the fact that the 2000 took several cues from the DS, even if customers chose to ignore the fact. The car sold well, especially the twin carburettor versions, and then there was the Buick-engined 3.5 litre V8 …

The Rover 2000 and siblings had interiors that were nearly as controversial as that of the DS. Angular in style, the 2000's instrumentation was housed in a box ahead of the steering wheel, and featured a strip-type speedometer; there were ergonomically-shaped rocker switches,

and good use was made of steering column-mounted, stalk-type controls. Tastefully furnished for the 'executive' customer, something quite new in marketing, the car featured sculptured rear seats trimmed in leather, and was designated as a four-seater luxury car instead of a five-seater.

BMC was also jealously looking over its shoulder at Citroën. The principles of hydrolastic suspension first seen in 1959 were encouraging, but nevertheless failed to achieve the comfort and compliancy of Citroën's hydropneumatics. Then there was front-wheel drive as endorsed by the Mini and 1100 series of models, later re-established with the much larger

1800s marketed as Austin, Morris, and Wolseley, according to trim specification. BMC engineering was the inspiration of Sir Alec Issigonis, one of the motor industry's most eminent designers. Issigonis made no secret of the fact that he held Citroën technology and engineering in high regard, and was an advocate of both *Traction Avant* and DS. Sir Alec once recalled that both cars - which he considered to be the most advanced in the world at the time - were used by BMC.

The bulky 1800 - with its uninspired styling and wheel-in-each-corner formula - was first seen in 1964; big on the inside with bags of space - more than any other British mass

produced car - this could well have been BMC's answer to the DS. Features included interconnected front and rear hydrolastic suspension, front disc brakes, rack and pinion steering, and cable-operated gear selection. Luxury arrived in 1967 in the shape of the Wolseley 18/85. In addition to the usual timber facia, round instruments and superior trim, there was optional automatic transmission with a facia-mounted selector and very welcome power steering. When the 2200 turned up in 1972 with its 105mph (169km/h) top speed it could have met the DS21 head-to-head, but didn't. Nor did the 110bhp Wolseley Six with its 6 cylinders and, oddly, 104mph (167km/h) speed maximum. The BMC cars did have their attributes: they accommodated six people - just - and enjoyed competent handling as long as power steering was employed. As for that bus-like driving position, least said the better.

The DS without rival? Well …

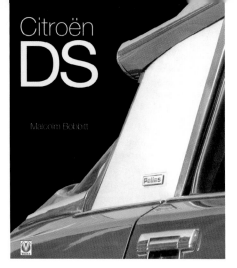

Citroën
DS

Malcolm Bobbitt

The SM was built using DS technology, combined with Maserati power and performance. (Courtesy Citroën)

For a long time after the war Citroën had wanted to market a true sporting grand tourer that would reflect the values of the *Grandes Routières*. There was deep regret amongst connoisseurs of fine motorcars that the great classic designs symbolising the elegance of prewar motoring had fallen into oblivion on two accounts: the decline of the bespoke coachbuilding industry, and the imposition of swingeing taxation on cars above 16CV - around

3 litres engine capacity. With the introduction of a taxation arrangement that made ownership of more powerful and expensive cars virtually impossible, famous marques like Bugatti, Delage, Delahaye, Hotchkiss, and Talbot-Lago fell into decline. Fortunately for Citroën the 15CV six-cylinder *Traction Avant* was below the tax break.

For the remainder of the *Traction* era and well into that of the *Dèesse*, Citroën produced cars that were

distinctly innovative, which appealed to a market unimpressed by Peugeot's staid engineering and Renault's failure to move from its middle-market position. Growing prosperity encouraged Citroën to offer a car even more prestigious than the DS *Pallas*,which filled the gap left by the ill-fated 22CV V8 of 1934.

THE MASERATI CONNECTION

Pierre Bercot seized the initiative to build a luxury grand tourer in 1964 when he instigated a development programme codenamed DS Sport. Within three years three prototype cars were built, each with engines developed from those used for production DSs. Tuning the DS19 engine pushed performance to nearly 110mph (177km/h), but it was the new five-bearing engine which showed real

results by boosting output from 90 to 130bhp to give 115mph (185km/h), and ultimately to 124bhp and 120mph (193km/h). There was, however, some dissatisfaction that progress centred around existing engines and familiar layouts, though a number of other engine configurations were researched.

The DS Sport programme took a dramatic new direction when Citroën courted Maserati in 1967 before fully absorbing the firm in March the following year. By using DS technology, Maserati power and in-house styling directed by Robert Opron, Citroën was able to devise a formidable luxury sports tourer. Citroën did not acquire Maserati purely in order to develop the SM but as part of a wider programme of expansion which anticipated proliferation of the Maserati marque.

First thoughts of designing a 'DS sports car' date from 1964, but it was not until 1967 that it became possible to blend Maserati and Citroën technology. This is the result, a superbly styled supercar. (Courtesy Citroën)

The formula for Citroën's grand tourer was enticing: a Citroën chassis with front-wheel drive, hydropneumatics controlling self-levelling suspension, all-round disc brakes and power steering, and the prestige and awesome power of a Maserati engine. The Sport Maserati - hence SM - development programme was established.

From the time that Maserati became part of the Citroën empire it was only two years before the SM was unveiled in March 1970 at the Geneva Motor Show. The choice of engine was paramount: ideally,

The SM was introduced in March 1970 at the Geneva Motor Show. The car's exquisite styling is evident here; notable features are the six-headlight system behind the massive glass canopy, and the hatchback design.
(Author's collection)

Maserati's V8 Indy 4136cc would have powered the car but it was physically too large, especially with front-wheel drive. There was also France's taxation levy to consider, which meant that anything above 2.8 litres was subject to a severe duty. A V6, rather than a V8, was therefore desirable; being shorter it fitted Citroën's chassis dimensions and was capable of being detuned to comply with the 16CV tax limit.

In charge of engine development was Maserati's chief engineer, Giulio Alfieri, who, having been asked to produce a suitable power unit delivering 150bhp within six months, had a V6 ready within three weeks. What Citroën got was a 200bhp engine,

The SM shared the DS's swivelling headlamp technology. Under the bonnet lies a 2670cc V6 engine which was designed in a matter of three weeks.
(Author's collection)

in essence a V8 Indy cut down to a 2670cc V6. When mated to Citroën's five-speed gearbox (positioned ahead of the engine) the unit was installed in a prototype 'cut-and-shut' DS, which featured faired-in headlamps, cut-away front wheelarches for use with wide section tyres, and reshaped rear wings to accommodate modified suspension designed for the SM.

The speed at which the SM was developed is apparent by how quickly the car was introduced. Much of the early testing was conducted using DS

mules - single headlamp models as well as the later types. Of particular importance were trials of Citroën's controversial powered steering system as originally devised by Paul Magès, and subsequently referred to as VariPower (in the UK) or Diravi (in France). Unlike other systems, VariPower, a feature of the Citroen CX as well as the SM, allowed the lightest of steering movements at low speeds, becoming heavier as progress quickened. While this arrangement was ideal, it did incorporate centre-point steering;

releasing the steering wheel allowed it to rapidly return to the straight-ahead position, a feature some motorists found disconcerting.

Robert Opron's styling for the SM has stood the test of time and, some thirty-five years since the design was unveiled, it remains stunningly exciting, aesthetically near perfect and aerodynamically proven in wind tunnel tests, with a drag coefficient as low as 0.39. Issuing from the same cradle as the *Traction Avant* and DS, anything less would have been unimaginable.

Unlike that of the DS, the SM's bodyshell, built by the specialist concern of Chausson, is a true monocoque, a massive structure that is vastly heavy by today's standards. The strength of the passenger cabin is such that with its load-bearing roof it forms a safety cage.

There were masterly touches about the SM's appearance, such as the nose with its full-width glass cowling concealing six *Cibié* headlamps, the innermost of each bank of three being long range and direction-controlled. Then there was the finely tapering shape of the body, together with an arresting side profile with a neat kick above the rear wheels, and the rear hatch elegantly marrying into the wings, which were welded, hence the need for detachable spats to aid wheel changing.

A car as finely shaped as the SM warrants interior styling beyond all expectation, and potential customers were not disappointed. It's necessary to appreciate Citroën's individualistic style to accept the dashboard arrangement; a throwback to Flaminio Bertoni's sculpture which graced the DS in its original form, now tastefully updated by Opron with instrumentation housed in oval dials: the single-spoke steering wheel was heavily padded. There were some surprises, too, like the uniquely shaped, supportive seats, and the central gearshift and lever-operated parking brake housed within a console, though there wasn't a transmission tunnel. The mushroom foot brake pedal required the lightest of pressure to activate awesome stopping power.

For a car as large as the SM - marginally longer than the DS though with a shorter wheelbase - it could reasonably be expected to have ample room for four people and their luggage. Citroën press release photographs are deceptive, showing a fur-clad model surrounded by bags of space. Rover advertising, too, used artistic licence to show a chauffeur loading suitcases into the boot of a Rover P4: either the compartment was oversized or the chauffeur was tiny! In fact, Citroën's publicity people purposely hired a model of particularly petite proportions to give the impression of there being considerably more room than was actually the case. The SM can only be described as a 2-plus-2, and luggage space is restricted, in fact, as the spare wheel is located in the boot above the large fuel tank rather than under the bonnet as it is on the DS. In practice, though, did anyone care? Not really, the SM was an expensive luxury sports coupé of such devastating performance that customers tended to ignore the practicalities.

LUXURY, AT A PRICE

Following its unveiling at Geneva the SM did not go on sale until August 1970. It was obviously intended as a limited production car, if only because of its price tag, which was twice that of the DS. At £5342 including tax, the SM was similarly priced to Aston Martin's DBS, Ferrari's Dino 246GT, the Mercedes 350SL, and Porsche 911S. A Jaguar E-type V12, on the other hand, cost nearly £1000 less. There were no right-hand drive production cars, but British customers were content with the few left hookers that trickled into Citroën's UK dealer network. There was a brave attempt by Middleton Motors of Potters Bar in north London to officially convert the SM to right-hand drive under Citroën contract, a complicated and expensive undertaking that was abandoned after only three cars had been prepared.

Motoring journalists clamoured to get their hands on the SM when it went on sale, if only to see if it really was capable of a top speed approaching 137mph (220km/h). *Autocar* and *Motor* testers were happy to achieve 135mph (217km/h), dispelling any misgivings they might have had about the VariPower steering. Not everyone was won over by the SM's performance, though: one leading magazine editor was openly hostile toward the car because he couldn't get used to its handling characteristics. Undoubtedly impressive was the car's ability to accelerate at such velocity that the driver was pressed back into the superbly shaped seat, and remarkable was the vehicle's stability, which was

The SM's cockpit. Superbly appointed, the SM featured manual or automatic transmission. The brake 'mushroom' can just be seen below the steering wheel; note the oval instruments. (Courtesy Citroën)

SM interior. Despite the car's generous proportions it is only a 2+2. (Courtesy Citroën)

obviously assisted by its aerodynamic perfection. On the subject of seats, the SM's - available with hide or Jersey upholstery - came in for some criticism for not giving sufficient lateral support when cornering hard, when the car had a tendency to roll rather more than might have been expected.

Press comment was mixed and ranged from sheer adoration to caution. The concensus of opinion was that it was fine on long sweeping bends and exhilarating on long straight roads, though some commentators

were less happy about negotiating twisting lanes, even though the car's suspension, firmer than that of the DS, gave a meticulous ride for those who appreciated the Citroën system.

During the SM's production career there were some important developments. From July 1971 Michelin supplied carbon fibre wheels which were considerably lighter in weight than the original steel type specially designed for the car. Both types of wheel, incidentally, were designed for use with Michelin's high performance XWX tyres. The following year fuel-injection became available, but not for the American market which received a 3-litre engine, triple carburettors and Borg-Warner fully automatic transmission. America-bound SMs were designed without the superlative

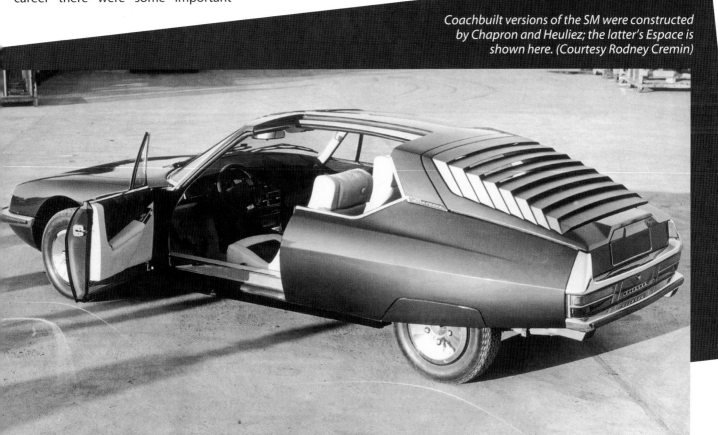

Coachbuilt versions of the SM were constructed by Chapron and Heuliez; the latter's Espace is shown here. (Courtesy Rodney Cremin)

lighting system given to cars for other markets - the FSS regulations insisting on four round sealed beam units and removal of that graceful glass cowling extending the width of the car's nose. What a shame!

Giulio Alfieri's Maserati V6 engine was a masterpiece of design but was not without its quirks. The camshaft drive system used duplex chains with a primary drive taken to the jackshaft in the vee of the engine. The primary chain was without adjustment, which meant that if the engine was over-revved the chain could jump a sprocket and cause extensive - and expensive - valve damage. With most owners aware of this potential problem the engine was modified by fitting an automatic tensioner to the primary chain.

The first two or so years of SM production were immensely satisfying

for Citroën, as a total of 9892 cars had been sold since August 1970. Then the oil crisis of 1973 struck and Pierre Bercot's aspirations for the SM began to fade. From 4988 cars sold in 1971, 4036 were built the following year before dramatically diminishing to a low of 2619 in 1973. In an attempt to reduce its liability, in early 1974 Citroën announced the transfer of SM production to Automobiles Ligier at Abrest near Vichy, where the specialist sports car firm built the Maserati-engined JS2. Production of the SM in 1974 amounted to 294 vehicles; 273 by Citroën in Paris and 21 by Ligier. In 1975 115 cars were constructed, 114 at Abrest.

If the SM dream wasn't already over, the final blow arrived in 1975. Peugeot had newly acquired Citroën and, in reviewing the model range,

The SM is as impressive from the rear as it is head-on. Sales of the car were immediately buoyant, until the fuel crisis of 1973, when they went into decline. In 1974 production of the car was transferred to Automobiles Ligier before being axed in 1975. (Courtesy Tony Stokoe/Brian Scott-Quinn)

had no hesitation in deciding that the gregarious and unashamedly luxurious SM was an indulgence. Production - and the Maserati affair - came to an immediate end.

For the record a total of 12,920 SMs were sold worldwide to an appreciative market. Few cars before or since have been so technically advanced, so invigorating to drive, and possessed of such character.

Citroën DS

Malcolm Bobbitt

In October 1955, just as the DS was being announced, the respected coachbuilder, Franay, presented President René Coty with this limousine built on the Citroën 15 Six H chassis. (Author's collection)

No sooner had the DS made its spectacular appearance at the 1955 Paris Salon, then the car attracted the attention of the French President, René Coty. For Coty, like Presidents before him, Citroën had become part of the French establishment. For Renault, France's state car manufacturer, that cars bearing the Double Chevron were favoured for Presidential use must have been difficult to bear, even though the Regie Nationale was without a suitable vehicle to offer for official or state purposes.

Before the DS the *Traction Avant* had served the Élysée Palace, and a glimpse into the Palace courtyard would have revealed an eclectic collection of vehicles. What better car to serve at official occasions than the seven- to eight-seater long wheelbase, 15-Six Familiale, or the luxurious 15 Six H? The Presidential cars commissioned by René Coty were grander than any before: a limousine designed by Philippe Charbonneaux and built in 1955 by Carrossier Franay, and a cabriolet built by Chapron in 1957, both of which were constructed on the 15-Six chassis. The late Michael Sedgwick makes the point in his excellent book, *The Motor Car 1946-56*, that the grandeur was somewhat superficial inasmuch that the Chapron vehicle comprised a number of components from other cars, such as Bentley door handles, a Buick rear

When HM The Queen visited France in 1957 the State Rolls-Royce Phantom IV was accompanied by a fleet of DS19s. (Author's collection)

window, Chevrolet rear lights, and a variety of Ford hardware. It was only a matter of time, therefore, before the DS replaced the *Traction Avant* for establishment use, demonstrated when HM the Queen made a state visit to France in October 1957, when the State Rolls-Royce Phantom 1V was accompanied by a convoy of DS19s.

One of the most ardent Citroën supporters was none other than Général Charles de Gaulle, President of France from 1959 until 1969. Often seen with a *Traction Avant*, de Gaulle's preferred mode of transport following his election as President was the DS, and he liked nothing better than to tour France in specially adapted examples that had removable fabric roofs - courtesy of coachbuilder Chapron and Paul Née - so he could stand upright and wave to the public. The DS rapidly became the official transport of government ministers and

civil servants, and black examples were a familiar sight in and around Paris.

The Goddess had a starring role in the epic film *The Day of the Jackal,* which chronicles an assassination attempt on Général de Gaulle. Part fact, part fiction, the film correctly describes how the DS's technical mastery saved the President's life. Sweeping out of Paris and approaching Petit Clamart to the south-west of the city in October 1961, the DS in which de Gaulle was travelling at 100km/h (62mph) was

Main picture & inset: Within the courtyard of the Élysée Palace a fleet of DSs on standby. (Author's collection)

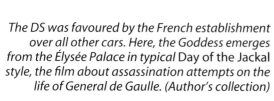

The DS was favoured by the French establishment over all other cars. Here, the Goddess emerges from the Élysée Palace in typical Day of the Jackal *style, the film about assassination attempts on the life of General de Gaulle. (Author's collection)*

DSs in attendance on a State occasion in France. (Author's collection)

ambushed by a gang of twelve armed men, the bullets from their rifles penetrating the coachwork of the President's car, as well as one of the rear tyres. De Gaulle's chauffeur, M. Marroux, accelerated from the scene at speed to safety, helped by the car's hydropneumatic suspension which compensated for the loss of stability caused by sudden tyre deflation. Had the President been travelling in any other type of car, the outcome would have been very different ...

A Grand DS

The two Presidential Citroëns commissioned by René Coty continued to be used for formal occasions until a new limousine was delivered to the Élysée Palace in 1968. A directive to supply a new Presidential limousine based on the DS was issued by Palace personnel in 1964 on behalf of Général de Gaulle, and a contract to construct the car was awarded to Carrossier Henri Chapron. In essence there was no other French coachbuilder with the same level of experience as Chapron. Heuliez was recognised for commercial vehicles, and it was not until the early 1970s that an involvement with cars began, which included the SM and specialisation in stretched limousines during the latter part of the decade. Franay had gone out of business, as had many other one-time leading coachbuilders.

During the 1960s and '70s official government DSs were a familiar sight in and around Paris. (Author's collection)

Coachbuilder Henri Chapron was commissioned to build a presidential DS in 1964, to be ready for delivery in 1968. This was no ordinary DS as it measured 6.55m (21ft 6in) in length and 2.13m (7ft 10in) in width. Général de Gaulle's one instruction was that it had to be longer than the American President's Lincoln! Built to the highest of standards, the car, nevertheless, disappointed de Gaulle, as he disliked the fixed interior division and was unhappy at not being able to converse easily with his chauffeur. The result was that he seldom used the DS, preferring instead the Franay-built car. (Courtesy Citroën)

Elsewhere, Frua of Italy remained in business, as did Mulliner Park Ward in Britain, by then incorporated within Rolls-Royce and Bentley Motor Cars. There was nobody more experienced to build de Gaulle's limousine, an assignment not without some difficulty.

De Gaulle had specified just one condition: his car should be longer than the US Presidential Lincoln. Work began but the Élysée Palace personnel failed to keep the President informed of progress, or give him the oppportunity to discuss his particular requirements for the interior. It had been left to the Palace staff to liaise with the coachbuilder and draw up a catalogue of design and mechanical features, amongst which was that the car should be capable of moving at a slow walking speed or ceremonial pace for several hours on end in hot weather without overheating. At 6.55 metres in length (21ft 6in) and 2.13 metres wide (7ft 10in) the car was huge by any standard, and weighed the equivalent of two production DSs. This gargantuan was powered by nothing more than the standard DS21 engine mated to a customary manual gearbox; there was, however, uprated cooling, suspension, braking and steering systems, full air conditioning, powered windows, refrigerator and cocktail cabinet. To cope with the electrical demand the power supply was effectively doubled by two heavy-duty batteries and two alternators. A particular requirement was a tight turning circle to allow the car to manoeuvre through the Élysée Palace gates from the rue Faubourg Saint-Honoré, negotiate the Palace courtyard, and stop at the steps, all in a single movement.

The two-tone metallic grey Presidential DS was certainly distinctive with its massive coachwork and long rear overhang. Add to this a deep windscreen and huge glass area, finest hide upholstery throughout, top quality veneers, and a rear compartment that was the epitome of luxury, and the DS was on a par with the Phantoms built for the British Royal Family. As for the DS's front compartment, this featured an impressive curved instrument board finished in wood and leather, and containing a plethora of dials and switches. The steering wheel was an adaptation of the familiar single-

These three images illustrate the styling of the Chapron Presidential DS, along with the car's generous proportions. (Courtesy Citroën)

spoke affair found on the regular DS. The exterior was also impressively styled, a particular feature being the twin headlamp system similar to that on later D models. Some of the styling had been instigated by Bertoni before he died, and was completed by Robert Opron.

The car delivered to the Élysée Palace had a vast, curved division with fixed rather than sliding glass, a feature which Paul Fontenil, then the President's chauffeur, knew would annoy de Gaulle. While the car was being finished at Chapron's coachworks Fontenil tried to have the division converted to a sliding glass type but his protestations went unheeded, largely because to do so would have been enormously difficult. De Gaulle was certainly not impressed when he saw the fixed division: he disliked using the car's microphone, preferring instead to have the division glass lowered in order to converse with his chauffeur. The Presidential DS car was seldom used by de Gaulle; on formal occasions the President elected instead to use the Franay 15-6 built for René Coty.

THE PRESIDENTIAL SMs

Thus, the magnificent DS Presidential Limousine remained mothballed for most of de Gaulle's Presidency, emerging only very occasionally. When Georges Pompidou became President of France he occasionally used the DS; that is until he took delivery of two exclusive Chapron SM cabriolets. For ceremonial duties when a cabriolet was required, the Élysée Palace had, since 1959, been reliant on two convertible V8 Simcas. The luxurious and comfortable SMs, therefore, were very welcome.

Following the SM's introduction in March 1970 it was only a matter of time before Henri Chapron offered a *Décapotable* version of the car, which was known as the Mylord and was displayed at the 1971 Paris Salon. Based on the production model, no more than seven cabriolets were built, all sharing the Coupé's overall dimensions. Another Chapron derivation of the SM was the Opéra, a strictly limited edition which was displayed at the 1972 Salon, where it attracted enormous attention. The Opéra was a long wheelbase four-door saloon version of the production SM coupé endowed with unashamed luxury and a 165,400FF price tag. Henri Chapron had already received a call from the Élysée Palace by the time the car made its appearance at the Salon: the President wanted two four-door SM cabriolets.

The Presidential SMs were based on the Mylord theme but were substantially lengthened to incorporate four doors instead of two, the experience developing the Opéra having proved useful. The cars featured hydraulically-operated hoods, and revised rear styling to that of the production coupés to allow a conventional boot lid rather than a rear hatch. At 18ft 4$^1/_2$in (5.60m) long with a wheelbase of 136.60in (3.47m), and weighing 35cwt (1778kg), the Presidential SMs were considerably larger than either the production car or the Mylord, and as a result featured modified suspension and braking, though the standard V6 engine and manual transmission were retained. For use on ceremonial occasions when the cars would be expected to undertake processional work over long periods of time, it was necessary to alter the final drive ratio, which meant that the top speed was limited to 112mph (180km/hr).

The Presidential SMs were delivered to the Élysée Palace in May 1972 and used on the occasion of HM The Queen's visit to France. Thirty-two years later when HM The Queen visited France again, the SMs were still in use.

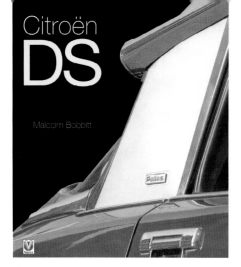

CHAPTER THIRTEEN

THE DS IN MOTORSPORT

Before the DS arrived the *Traction Avant* had proved itself a credible performer in events such as the Paris-Nice Rally, providing stiff competition to BMWs and Peugeots, amongst others. When it came to negotiating snow and ice, the front-wheel drive Citroën often led the field in events that included the formidable Lyon-Charbonnières, Monte Carlo, and Coup des Alpes. The *Traction's* abilities were ably demonstrated by François Lecot in 1935-6 when he covered 400,134 kilometres (248,631 miles) in 369 days as a wager.

No sooner had the DS made its debut than Citroën's publicity people were busy preparing for the car's baptism of fire on the rally circuit by participating in the 1956 Monte Carlo Rally with six privately owned cars with company support. A single DS19, crewed by Paul Coltelloni and Pierre Alexandre, finished the event and was placed seventh overall, and was outright winner of the 2-litre class: Citroën lost no time in promoting these achievements.

The DS was still very much in its infancy, and there had been little time in which to perfect handling techniques and acclimatise to the car's hydropneumatic system under rally conditions. Not that the hydraulics failed in any way: the suspension, steering and braking systems proved themselves beyond doubt, but the semi-automatic transmission took some getting used to, especially in perfecting rapid gear changes, which resulted in the crew destroying the gearbox by the time the car arrived at Monte Carlo. Despite the 1956 Monte result and the good publicity it had generated, Citroën was nevertheless reluctant to further its involvement in motorsport until quite sure that the DS could take the laurels.

Citroën's decision to withdraw from competitive events for a period did not prevent the DS taking part unofficially, and enjoying some notable successes, such as in the 1957 Swedish Rikspo Kalen, the Mille Miglia, and the 1958 Coupe des Alpes. Citroën officially returned to rallying in 1959 and immediately won the Monte Carlo team entry with the ID19, which was considered better equipped for motorsport than its more complicated sibling. Despite a lower power output compared to the DS19, the ID19's manual transmission and non-powered steering compensated in terms of performance - until, that is, the manually-operated DS19 arrived.

SPORTING ACHIEVEMENTS

Citroën's 1959 Monte Carlo success - courtesy of drivers Coltelloni, Alexandre, and Desrosiers - was the beginning of a year of achievement. René and Mme Trautmann took first place in the Criterium Neige et Glace 1600-2000cc touring class category with their ID19, whilst Leal and Chevron, in a DS19, were placed first in the over 1600cc sports car class. Paul Coltelloni and co-driver Desrosiers secured first place in the 1600-2000cc touring class Acropolis Rally driving an ID19, a punishing 1900 mile (3058km) event comprising difficult hilly and unmade roads. This was a precursor to

Paul Coltelloni pictured in 1959 with his ID19 after winning that year's Monte Carlo Rally. Later Coltelloni was honoured as Rally Champion of Europe. (Courtesy Citroën)

the five-day Coupe des Alpes, in which competitors were required to negotiate some 100 mountain passes, including the formidable Lautaret, Galibier, and Mont Revard. Coltelloni and Desrosiers were again placed first with their ID19 in the 1600-2000cc touring class. Paul Coltelloni was also successful in the Adriatic Rally with his ID19, this time with Houel as co-driver. Then Coltelloni, with Desrosiers co-driving, stormed to victory in the Viking, Marathon de la Route, and Deutschland rallies with the ID19. While Coltelloni and Desrosiers were collecting trophies around Europe, Simonetti and Marchetti were promoting Citroën with their ID19, taking the laurels in the 1-2 litre touring class Tour de Corse.

The DS and ID had became familiar but formidable contenders in motor sport and had enjoyed successive

Though lower powered than DS19s, some rally drivers preferred the ID19 with its manual transmission and non-hydraulic steering. Citroën took first, third and fifth placings in the Liège-Sofia- Liège rally of 1961 when only eight of the original 85 competitors finished. Here, the winning car - driven by Lucien Bianchi and Georges Harris - storms to victory. (Courtesy Citroën)

victories in some events. The DS was placed first in the 1600-2000cc normal touring class of the Monte in 1961 and 1962, and DS19s dominated the 1963 Monte Carlo, placed 2nd, 4th, 5th, 7th and 10th in general classification, this result winning for Citroën the Coupe des Constructeurs. DS19s took 3rd and 1st places in general classification for 1962 and 1963 in Finland's demanding Hanki Rally, and took the field between 1960 and 1964 (1963 excepting) competing at the Criterium Niege et Glace. Snow and ice gave the DS and ID a distinct advantage over most cars, the surety of front-wheel drive combined with hydropneumatic suspension giving them a lead during the Norwegian Rallies of 1962-3.

Highlights of the DS's sporting successes include the years between 1960 and 1964 when Citroën featured prominently in the Lyon/ Charbonnières/Stuttgart Rally, the Coupe des Alpes, and the Marathon de la Route, the latter undoubtedly among the toughest of all European road endurance events. Before 1961 the Marathon de la Route was considered particularly challenging with its Liège-Rome-Liège section, but then the Liège-Sofia-Liège route demanded four days and nights of continuous driving along the length of Yugoslavia over the worst roads of Europe. Of the 85 cars that entered the 1961 event only eight finished, three of which were DS19s, placed 1st (Lucien Bianchi and Georges Harris), 3rd (R. Neyret and J. Terramorsi), and 5th (Lageneste and Burglin). Twenty cars out of 119 entrants finished the 1962 event; five DS19s, four of which were among the first ten, to give Citroën the Coupe des Constructeurs. History repeated itself in the 1964 event when four DS19s among the first twelve of twenty-one finishers - from a field of 106 competing cars - won for Citroën the Coupe des Constructeurs, and for France the Trophee des Nations.

RENÉ COTTON'S INFLUENCE
The inspiration behind Citroën's rallying successes was René Cotton, who was pressed into managing Citroën's newly-formed competitions department by Jacques Wolgensinger, the firm's enterprising PR chief. Initially Cotton declined to take on the job as it meant sacrificing his independence as a freelance motor sports promoter. Refusing to accept defeat, Wolgensinger persuaded Citroën and Cotton to come to an agreement whereby Citroën would supply vehicles to Cotton as team entries and finance all preparation.

René Cotton's influence on the Citroën team, in terms of both cars and drivers (Cotton was responsible for recruiting some of the marque's best drivers) is evidenced by the DS's success on the rally scene.

However, the DS did not excel in situations where speed was of the essence, but under the harshest conditions the DS and ID came into their own, their mechanical specification ensuring that however bad the road surface, or severe the weather conditions - or even a combination of both - they were able to continue where others could not. The DS and ID's hydraulic system proved their saviour on many an occasion: when the terrain was very tough it was an easy matter to gain ground clearance by adjusting suspension height, and when there was no time to stop and change a punctured tyre, again, adjust the suspension to high and carry on with three wheels! Drivers quickly adapted to the techniques necessary to handle the DS and compensate for lag in changing gear ratios by synchronized use of brake and throttle. And then there was knowing how to control the car's understeer most effectively by braking before a corner, but then accelerating through it in order to shift the weight from the front to the rear wheels to keep as tight a course as possible. Of the car's many attributes, though, it was its total comfort that was particularly appreciated by crews as it noticeably reduced driver and co-driver fatigue when compared to other vehicles.

Citroën entered a team of six

cars for the 1965 East African Safari, attracting drivers of calibre such as Lucien Bianchi, Oliver Gendebien, Guy Verrier, Patrick Vanson, and Jean Claude Ogier. With five DSs among the seventeen finishers from out of more than ninety entrants, it was Volvo, Peugeot, Ford, and Mercedes that took the first four places, fifth going to Citroën with Bianchi and Jeeves, and eighth to Verrier and Vanson.

A HOLLOW VICTORY

When Citroën entered the 1966 Monte Carlo Rally there was nothing to

Bianchi and Ogier en route to Australia in the 1968 London-Sydney Marathon. In sight of victory, a Mini collided with the car, seriously injuring Bianchi. (Courtesy Rodney Cremin)

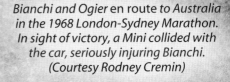

suggest that the result would be highly contentious, sufficiently so to sour Anglo-French motor industry relations for some considerable time. In practice the team of DS21s did reasonably well, six of the eight Citroëns finishing within the first fifteen places. When the result of the event was declared, the DS had done rather better than expected, with Pauli Toivonen's DS21 placed first.

Imagine the furore that ensued when first place was awarded not to Timo Makinen but to Toivonen's DS21,

Bianchi's and Ogier's DS performed admirably throughout the London-Sydney Marathon, and required nothing more serious than routine maintenance, until, that is, the car was wrecked a few miles from the finish. (John Reynolds collection)

continued page 168

Main pic & inset: Citroën won outright the 1969 Rallye du Maroc. Note the cut-away rear wings to ease wheel changing. (Courtesy Citroën)

These two graphic photographs give some idea of the conditions rally cars were expected to endure. Citroën's hydraulic suspension proved itself beyond all doubt on such events. (Courtesy Citroën)

For rallying purposes Citroën built DS coupés similar to that shown in these two photographs, which were made using the 'cut-and-shut' method. Driven by Neyret and Terramorsi, such a car was successful in the 1969 Rallye du Maroc. (Courtesy Citroën)

Top right: This ID20 was the sole survivor in the 1969 Tour de Portugal. (Courtesy Citroën)

Right & overleaf: Australian drivers Jim Reddiex and Ken Trubman celebrate winning the 1974 UDT World Cup Rally in a largely unmodified DS. At the time Reddiex was Brisbane's Citroën dealer; following his success the car became something of a celebrity in Australia. (Courtesy Martin Thomas)

following disqualification of BMC's Mini Coopers which had finished first, second, and third overall. The British press was outraged at what was seen as a deliberate attempt by the French to deny victory to the BMC team for what, it was alleged, was a minor lighting infringement. The

Minis' headlamps had single filament bulbs, so dipped beams had to be provided by auxiliary lamps, which, it was argued, contravened regulations. Whilst Citroën was awarded victory, it was a hollow one, to say the least, as the BMC Minis were seen as victims of a calculated campaign against them. The Minis had their revenge in the 1967 Monte, enjoying a convincing victory, leaving first in class for the DS21 to win for Citroën.

LONG DISTANCE RALLYING

It was soon after the Monte Carlo tussle with the Mini Coopers that Citroën's policy changed to concentrate on long distance rallying, which better suited the DS. Of these the most spectacular was the 1968 London-Sydney Marathon for which three DSs were entered, one privately, the other two by Citroën.

The two Citroën-entered cars were prepared in Britain at the company's Slough workshops as part of a works team, Lucien Bianchi and Jean Claude Ogier driving one car; Neyret and Terramorsi crewing the other. The itinerary was formidable to say the least: non-stop driving for more than 10,000 miles (16,093km) via twelve countries, to be completed within 250 hours. By the time the cars had reached Australia, 72 of the 98 that had set out remained, with a number having to be substantially rebuilt in India. The DS21s had performed admirably, and had not required any repairs since their London departure, thus helping to put Bianchi and Ogier in third place as they set off

Tony Mather and his son competing in the 2003 Winter Challenge in their DS23. In recent years the DS has become a recognised favourite with rally enthusiasts, noted for its durability and comfort. (Courtesy Tony Mather)

from Freemantle on their rush across Australia to Sydney. It was during this stage of the rally that Bianchi and Ogier managed to move up to first place, and on the final leg of the journey increased their lead over the Rootes Motors Hillman Hunter driven by Andy Cowan, and Paddy Hopkirk, who was in third place driving a BMC 1800.

An hour or so and 100 miles (161km) from certain victory, disaster struck. Ogier was driving the final leg as Bianchi slept, secure in the certain knowledge that their DS21 would be first to cross the finish line, when a Mini appeared on the road ahead, swerving from side to side. It hit the Citroën head-on, badly injuring Bianchi who

was thrown into the windscreen, his legs trapped beneath the dashboard. Paddy Hopkirk was soon on the scene and helped release the Citroën's crew, as well as ensuring that petrol leaking from the Mini did not ignite.

Subsequent rallies included the 1969 Rallye du Maroc. Of the 78 cars that left Rabat, seven were DSs, five of which were entered by Citroën, one being a 'shut-and-cut' coupé driven by Neyret and Terramorsi. The going was so tough that by the time Marrakesh was reached there were just twenty-one survivors. Only seven cars reached the finish line at Casablanca; five DSs led by Neyret and Terramorsi, the other two Renaults. For Citroën

Tony Mather from Northumberland changing a wheel on his DS 23 whilst competing in the Inca Rally in South America. Few cars require the rear wing to be removed in order to change a tyre! Note that the car's suspension height has been raised to facilitate wheel removal. Tony is a regular competitor around the world in his DS. (Courtesy Tony Mather)

the rally was a walkover: first in general classification; first in team classification, and winner of the Coupe des Constructeurs.

When, in 1969, Citroën entered the Tour de Portugal, it was an ID20 that made it to the winning line, the sole car left in the event, the rest of the field having withdrawn at various intervals. The following year Citroën failed to achieve better than seventh place in the London-Mexico, and in 1973 (by which time Marlène Cotton took over Citroën's competition department following the death of her husband,

René) four DS23s entered the Rallye du Maroc to finish second overall.

The final event in which the DS took the laurels was the 1974 UDT World Cup Rally. Prepared by Citroën, all of the DSs entered finished the rally, the only manufacturer to be able to make this claim; the winning car was driven by Australians, Jim Redddiex and Ken Trubman, the former having operated Brisbane's Citroën franchise for a number of years. Naturally, the car became a celebrity in its home country, and whenever it appeared at motoring events it was greeted rapturously.

At the time of Citroën's UDT World Cup Rally victory the DS was at the end of the road: the rally mantle had been taken up by the SM, which won the 1971 Rallye du Maroc, and the same year an SM-engined DS won the Niege et Glace.

Thirty years after going out of production the DS is often seen competing in classic events around the world, claiming, as might be expected, splendid victories in the hands of enthusiastic owners.

Citroën

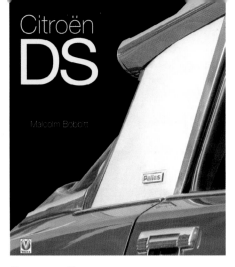

Citroën
DS

Malcolm Bobbitt

CHAPTER FOURTEEN
LIVING WITH THE GODDESS

The Goddess is equally at home negotiating city streets, wafting gracefully along wide, poplar-lined roads, or tearing around hairpin bends high up in the Alps or Pyrenees. Those nervous of lifting her bonnet, or peeping under her hemline, can be reassured by the fact that, contrary

This is not what most potential DS buyers see when looking under the bonnet of a car: this is Tony Mather's DS23 which he uses for rallying. Tony has removed the spare wheel from its usual forward position and laid the radiator flat, having installed twin cooling fans. The picture does show the under-bonnet layout of the DS with its hydraulic complexity - this is a semi-automatic car - along with the position of the engine, which is set well back. (Author's collection)

Beware the temptation of a barn find or a car which has been languishing in a field for some considerable time. Whilst restoring such a vehicle might be feasible, it will require great expense and expertise to get it back on the road. (Author's collection)

to popular belief, she is actually very practical.

BUYING ADVICE

DS owners will be used to the attention their cars receive, and will have suffered many remarks about 'funny suspension'. However, the DS's

How to tell a car's age: this is an early example, pre-1963 model year. (Author's collection)

A post September 1962 car pictured in Sydney in 1978. While it has 'single' headlamps, it has the face-lifted nose which remained in vogue until September 1967. Australian market Ds were supplied from Slough until they were built locally. The opening of Citroën assembly plants in Australia and South Africa contributed to the cessation of assembly in Britain. (Author's collection)

Single headlamp Ds are now relatively rare; this Pallas was photographed in Amsterdam in 2002. Holland has many DS enthusiasts and, as a result, much expertise in restoring vehicles. Look closely at the front wing that is damaged: because of the DS's construction it's an easy task to remove the wing in order to make repairs. (Courtesy H. John Black)

rallying successes should be sufficient to convince even the most cynical that hydropneumatic suspension is stronger and far more compliant than steel springs, and, having been around for more than fifty years, has been used under licence by other manufacturers.

For those who have fallen under the DS's spell, all that remains is to find a suitable car. Should it be left- or right-hand drive? Then there's the choice between older models with single headlamps, or the later, twin headlamp type, and the relatively simplified ID or the more luxurious - and arguably more complex - DS.

Left-hand or right-hand drive is a matter of personal preference; some enthusiasts are advocates of the early model's design purity. Obviously, there will be greater numbers of left-hand drive vehicles from which to choose, simply because right-hand drive examples were built for specific markets, including the British Commonwealth. A popular way of locating a particular car is to scour classified advertisements, and the internet. After Britain, France is the obvious place to begin the search, where the car enjoys a healthy following with plenty of specialists offering good quality cars. Finding a DS wearing an *A vendre* label parked outside a rural property could be just too tempting ...

The biggest market for the DS outside its native country is Holland where there is a wealth of restoration expertise and component supply, whether original or re-manufactured.

For reasons of age alone, fewer early cars - those with single or 'frog-eye' headlamps - are available than the later 'shark-front' models. The earliest types, those produced before the first face-lift, are now quite rare. These cars, unless they have been converted to 'green' LHM hydraulic fluid, will use 'red' LHS fluid, so take this into account when considering such an example. Red fluid is readily available from specialist suppliers but is expensive and extremely hygroscopic. If corrosion to the hydraulic system pipework is to be avoided a car's fluid should be changed regularly. Beware of cars that have stood unused for long periods as 'red system' components can seize due to inactivity. Because red fluid is corrosive, spillage on the car's paintwork can have disastrous results.

Some owners of older cars have forsaken originality for practicality by converting their car's hydraulic system to accept green fluid. This is a painstaking task which is not cheap since all hydraulic components have to be changed or modified. Such projects could entail fitting new pipework and are therefore best attempted when the car is undergoing restoration. It is, nonetheless, a worthwhile modification since cars converted to LHM do provide peace of mind for owners, and, contrary to belief, there's little difference in ride quality. Always check the hydraulic fluid on older cars: vehicles which have been converted should have green reservoirs; red fluid cars will have black reservoirs.

Whilst older cars have a charisma all their own, performance is not as spirited as in later cars, though driving is no less pleasurable. Take care when examining early Ds since they will usually have amassed very high mileages, and may have undergone substantial mechanical and bodywork repairs. For someone without extensive knowledge of these cars who is considering a purchase, it would be wise to have the vehicle inspected by a marque expert. The fee for such a service could well be a good investment and save later cost and disappointment.

There are four ways of buying a DS: through a specialist, classic car dealer, at auction, or a private sale. You should have little difficulty sourcing vehicles through reputable specialists, the advantage here being assurance that a car is properly presented, with as full a history as possible, details of work carried out prior to sale, current MoT test certificate, and guarantee. The asking price will undoubtedly be higher than for a car offered privately, but once the purchase has been completed and you're enjoying the car, the premium paid will soon be forgotten. For advice about reputable specialists, ask other enthusiasts, or join the Citroën Car Club.

Buying at auction is a recipe for disaster unless you know exactly what to look for. Classic car dealers often acquire their stock at auction, so extreme care should be taken when contemplating such a purchase. There are some very reputable dealers but others have little knowledge about cars as idiosyncratic as the DS. Private sales can be risky; the following is intended as a brief guide of what to expect when viewing a car.

Unless potential owners are determined to find an early car, most will choose to purchase a late model with faired-in headlamps. It pays to purchase the best example you can find, as the price premium will soon be forgotten. Buying a vehicle to a tight budget could lead to disappointment. When looking at later models decide whether you want a DS, D Super or D Spécial: each will have different trim and equipment levels. (Author's collection)

When viewing a car it's prudent to carry out a number of checks to establish its true condition. This Safari is obviously a working car and shows signs of wear and tear. The offside front wing carries masking tape, and there's visible corrosion on the door bottoms. The interior of the car is likely to be worn, so check whether it's still serviceable.
(Courtesy H. John Black)

PRE-PURCHASE CHECKLIST

First impressions when viewing a car are important, and unless you are very objective, can cloud your judgement. A clean car inside and out might initially appear good value - until one takes a more critical look. Having checked the car's exterior for visible signs of damage or corrosion, lift the bonnet (which should be free from cracks and aluminium corrosion) by pulling the bonnet release located beneath the passenger side of the dashboard, and then releasing the safety catch beneath the bonnet's leading edge on the driver's side. (According to model, some cars will be fitted with two interior bonnet releases each side of the cabin.) Take care to secure the bonnet by locating the stay in the socket on the side of the engine compartment. Feel the radiator and engine for signs of the car having been run before your arrival; it's best if it's cold as starting the engine will give a clear indication of overall mechanical condition. At this stage check that the oil is clean and the level correctly shown between the two marks on the dipstick. Check hydraulic and coolant levels.

For easy starting from cold early models will require petrol to be hand-pumped to the carburettor; the pump is located on the right-hand side of the engine near the dipstick. The battery should be capable of providing sufficient power without appearing to discharge. Having set the suspension to its highest position, start the engine - it should run and idle evenly - closing the choke as soon as possible. Check the exhaust for blue smoke - hopefully there'll be none - and see how long it takes for the car to rise: up to thirty seconds or so depending on the length of time the vehicle has been inactive. Expect to hear the high pressure pump in action: when the car is at full height it will cut out with a definite click and then cut in again every twenty seconds or so. If a pump operates continuously suspect that the main accumulator sphere needs replacing; exchange spheres can be obtained from Citroën hydraulic specialists. Another test is to depress the brake pedal several times in quick succession, then after a minute or so rapidly rotate the steering wheel from side to side a dozen times. Neither of these actions should cause the pump to operate, but if they do it's a further sign that the accumulator sphere requires attention.

Now turn your attention to the cooling system: check for water leaking from the radiator, water pump and hoses. With the suspension in the raised

The area around front wheelarches is prone to corrosion on a DS, a clear indication that repair work is urgently required if major surgery and expense are to be avoided. (Author's collection)

position and the engine at rest, check for hydraulic fluid leaks, taking extreme care not to place yourself beneath the car unless it is properly supported on wooden blocks or secured on a proper vehicle lift. Check also for evidence of oil around the engine sump, particularly the oil filter cover, which, if excessive, suggests poor fitment of the filter.

Take a look along the bottom of the car, checking for signs of corrosion. Door bottoms rot, which mean that, at best, repair sections can be grafted into place, and, at worst, complete new doors will have to be sourced. Look at the sills each side of the car; don't try and remove the covers concealing the hydraulic pipework but do feel for a lip along the length of the outer edge. If there's slight movement don't worry; this is how it should be. When there is no appreciable movement or the lip is not perceptible, it's likely that a repair has been attempted. Likewise, if the underside of the sill shows signs of damage this indicates corrosion problems. Check, too, for signs of corrosion along the car's underbody, in particular around the boot floor area which can corrode at the edges and the forward end in line with the rear door pillars. Rot here will require immediate attention for this is the base of the

transverse box section, the outer limits of which support the rear suspension components.

Having now lowered the D's suspension to normal running height, open the boot, checking the closing edge of the lid for rot before taking a look inside the compartment. Early signs of corrosion caused by water ingress will be evident; repairs will be required sooner or later, including removal of the fuel tank. To get a better idea of a car's condition, remove the rear wings by undoing the single retention bolt on each. Wings are prone to rusting where they fit against the rear doors, as are the top sections which fit adjacent to the boot lid; inspect the inner rear wings, rear suspension, and bumper mountings for signs of rot.

Now turn your attention to the roof, which will be made of fibreglass or aluminium. Look for signs of water ingress around the headlining, if fitted, and beware of excessive sealant around the external seam. Check the front footwells for obvious signs of water seepage, usually the result of leaking roof joints, poorly fitting doors and windows, and/or leaking windscreen surround. Aluminium roofs tend to degenerate at the edges, hence copious amounts of mastic. It will be virtually

impossible to source an aluminium roof in good condition, so one that is showing signs of corrosion will have to be replaced with a fibreglass version.

When inspecting the front of the vehicle there shouldn't be any signs of rot around the wheelarches, the rear of the inner wings or wing mounting points. Ensure there's no sign of corrosion around the headlamps and front valence, and on Slough cars take a look at the rectangular number plate box, which should be sound. Locating a replacement number plinth won't be easy, and fabricating a new one will be costly and time-consuming. Particular points to inspect are body trim items: Pallas models were furnished with side rubbing strips with rubber inlay along the crease line of the doors, extending to the wings (with corrosion-prone fixing points); stainless steel beading adorned the top of the doors and was fitted to wing and door bottoms. Sill trims were also fitted with cut-outs for jacking points.

Check tyre condition (including the spare wheel which sits ahead of the radiator), which, ideally, should be Michelin X on older models and XAS on later types. Uneven tyre wear can indicate poor tracking or wheel balance. Carefully examine tyre walls

This tired-looking DS needs some care and attention if it is to be saved from complete dilapidation. The paintwork has seen better days, the door panels no longer fit as they should, and the wheelarches are showing signs of corrosion, all of which suggest that some elements of mechanical components will probably require attention, too. If considering the purchase of a car like this, bear in mind that a specialist might be needed to complete the necessary restoration. (Author's collection)

for signs of damage or malformation through standing idle for very long periods. The stand used to raise a car when changing wheels should be located with the spare wheel; ensure the wheel brace is with the car. Check, too, that the centre wheel fixing nut is in good condition and without rounded edges. A worn fixing will make wheel changing difficult, to say the least.

Inspect the windscreen, which should be scratch-free, and the condition of the wiper blades. Early Ds have wipers which sweep outwards from the centre base of the screen, so leave a central part of the glass unswept. Examine headlamp lenses, reflectors and bulbs. Older French cars will have 6-volt electrics and may well have yellow lamps fitted. Some early Ds were fitted with auxiliary lamps, which are nice period pieces, but check that they operate correctly. Shark-front Ds may have directional long range lamps, in which case the swivelling mechanism should be in perfect working order.

THE COMFORT ZONE

It should be appreciated that there are differing levels of interior trim, from the more utilitarian fabrics specified for the ID models, to the luxury materials used for DS and Pallas models. Because a car is offered with DS or Pallas trim it does not necessarily mean that it will be genuine. A number of IDs, D Spécials and D Supers have been refurbished with *Pallas* seats and trim, so a vehicle might not be quite what it seems ... The condition of a car's interior will

be immediately apparent: beware of damaged fabric, whether cloth, vinyl (referred to as Targa) or hide, as these can be expensive to repair properly. Cars with cloth upholstery can suffer from faded or threadbare front and rear backrests, whilst Targa splits along the seams. Leather upholstery should be regularly treated with hide feed to keep it supple and prevent cracking. In all cases seats should be in good condition without unsightly stains or burns, and free from sagging: door panels should also be clean and damage-free. When looking at elderly IDs don't dismiss those cars which have a particular aroma that is associated with cloth material and rubberised floor coverings - it's common to a lot of vehicles.

Carpeting should be clean, dry, and without holes. More expensive models were treated to thick carpet underlay and can absorb moisture. Any sign of dampness should be carefully investigated. Seats should easily move in their runners and back rests function correctly. Steering wheels on early cars will have slim rims bound in black wear-resistant material, though white binding was reserved for Slough vehicles. Late models have padded wheels which become shiny and slippery with age but shouldn't show signs of damage. If a steering wheel cover is fitted take a peep at the condition of the material underneath. It goes without saying that the facia should be in good condition with all instruments and switches operational.

Check mirrors, sun visors, door handles and catches. Don't be afraid to sit in all the seats, check for comfort, and make a critical analysis of the vehicle's overall condition.

Before we proceed to more in-depth matters a few words about the Slough-built cars, very few of which have survived. Because of their rarity a Slough car in good condition can command higher than average prices. The trim on ID models was superior to that of French cars with quality hide, and equal to the DS, though dashboard arrangements differed by way of wooden facias and unique controls and instrumentation. Slough cars were always equipped with 12-volt electrics, which means that some fittings, such as rear indicator and lamp lenses, are different to their French counterparts.

THE MECHANICAL ELEMENT

It is essential to carefully check a car's provenance, and to do this compare chassis number and model type (found on a plate fixed to the left-hand bulkhead, as viewed from the front of the car) to that shown on the registration and MoT documents. Compare these with the chassis number stamped on the centre of the bulkhead and concealed by a rubber seal. Engine numbers can also be checked (find the plate on the left-hand side of the crankcase adjacent to the gearbox bellhousing), but remember that engines can be swopped ...

Test all electrical items and the charging system. It is possible to fit

Early Ds will have centre-fixing wheels, as depicted here. Ensure that the hexagonal fitting is in good condition, and is not damaged or rounded, which can make wheel removal difficult. Evident here is the inboard braking; check that all driveshaft gaiters are sound and not split. (Courtesy Citroën)

electronic ignition to even the earliest models, the IDs having manual advance and retard. Check that the accelerator and clutch pedals operate smoothly (if fitted), the ease with which the gear selector slides, and the parking brake travel. Early cars have an unusual adjustment calling for use of a special tool, something owners will not usually have in their possession. Parking brake adjustment on these models is far from easy and will normally require specialist attention. A D's brakes are powerful but nevertheless those at the rear can seize due to lack of use, especially if the car carries little weight. The fuel system should be carefully examined for leaks, especially the feed to the carburettor by checking the soundness of the hose connections.

Look for signs that the car has been properly maintained, either from service records or indications that greasing and oiling has been regularly done. Finally, check out the heating

A car's provenance should be carefully checked - do this by establishing that chassis and engine numbers agree with vehicle documentation. Beware of cars which have been involved in accidents; not all accident damage will result in a car being written off, so checking that steering and other mechanical items are in good order is essential. Accident damage may not appear extensive, but will still be expensive and time-consuming to repair. (Author's collection)

Cabriolets are highly sought-after, especially right-hand drive examples. Because there were only fifty Décapotables officially imported into the United Kingdom the cars have a price premium. A car in this condition will require complete restoration, which is going to be very expensive. (Courtesy Tony Stokoe/Brian Scott-Quinn)

and ventilation system, and establish that the controls are working and the thermostat dial on the firewall is not seized.

When looking at a Safari some particular points should be borne in mind: all cars have steel roofs, the tailgate can show signs of corrosion around the panel below the glass - and don't forget to test the hinges for security. Remember that it's not possible to remove the rear wings, so check carefully for signs of corrosion in this area. It's likely that Safaris have been used to carry bulky loads so check that trim items are undamaged. Examine occasional seats and check they're operational and in good condition.

Cabriolets are also a special case and care should be taken to establish that vehicles are sound and free from corrosion, especially the rear section which takes the weight of the hood. More than anything else check the car's provenance: a number of so-called Décapotables are actually conversions. There are, however, some exceptional conversions on the market which have been prepared by reputable specialists, but remember that these are not genuine Chapron cars.

THE TEST DRIVE
Ease yourself into the mode of driving a DS. On semi-auto cars flick the gear selector into first, feel the transmission take up as the accelerator is depressed; ease off the right foot, shift into second ... third ... top ... easy! Test the brakes,

gently, for the mushroom requires just the lightest pressure. There shouldn't be any snatching of gears, nor jolting as the brake is applied. Cars with power steering will enable finger-tip control so take care to acclimatise to the lightness of the steering.

Manual transmission cars will require a different approach. The steering on early model IDs without power assistance is painfully heavy at low speeds and when parking. Under way, however, the steering is light. Be prepared to make relaxed gear changing; the column change is delightfully light but lethargic. Cars without power brakes will require a lot of pedal effort, and don't forget that ID19s with their lower power output require much gear work, especially over hilly terrain.

DS21 and 23s have levels of performance far superior to DSs and ID19s. They feel more modern, too, but lack the special character of the early machines. Driving at speed, engine and road noise is evident, and expect some whistling or air around the front windows. The car should ride evenly with just a hint of road surface awareness; anything else will indicate that suspension spheres require renewal. Expect to hear a series of wheezes as the car negotiates uneven surfaces or humpback bridges - this is the hydraulic system in operation.

Steering should be precise; wandering or a need for constant correction will indicate track rod wear.

At a low speed put the steering on full lock - some pulsating will be felt through the steering wheel. Listen for knocking sounds which are a sign that the driveshafts are worn. Fuel-injected cars will have exhilarating performance but even models with twin choke carburettors will out-perform many 2-litre cars. Water temperature of around 75-78 degrees C should be maintained; the comprehensive instrument display warning lamps on late model vehicles with the black slab dashboard should not be illuminated. All-in-all, it should be the best drive you've ever experienced!

SO YOU'VE BOUGHT A DS!
Maintaining a DS is quite straight-forward, although many owners will prefer that a specialist look after the car for them. There's no problem with this as there are many independent Citroën specialists.

The DS does have its foibles, to be sure, and the clutch cable on manual transmission cars can break with wear, so it's a good idea to keep a spare one in the tool kit. Always keep a spare fan belt, along with bulbs and sparkplugs.

Even DSs deteriorate with age and wear, and the time may come when serious conservation work is necessary. Choose the specialist carefully, let them see the vehicle before entrusting the work to them, talk about the time it will take to complete and, just as important, the cost of the work. Discuss whether originality is the main criteria, or whether modifications should be made to make the vehicle more acceptable to today's traffic conditions. (This

Cars such as this, photographed at the Beaulieu Autojumble, are obviously not genuine cabriolets. Nevertheless, such vehicles can give enjoyable motoring as long as the conversion work has been carefully undertaken.
(Author's collection)

might include changing from red fluid to green, fitting a DS 21 or 23 engine in place of a worn DS or ID19 unit, fitting halogen lamps, or re-trimming the car with new and more comfortable seats.)

An essential aspect of ownership is talking with other enthusiasts, sharing knowledge and becoming more confident about these fine vehicles. The DS, whether an early or late model, is an eminently usable car which should be driven and not laid up as a museum piece. Enthusiasts use them for rallying, everyday driving, and just for the pleasure of it. They are no more prone to wear and tear than any other car - just remember to carry out routine servicing. The DS was a very advanced car which looks more modern than some more recent vehicles, but bear in mind that the earliest examples are at least fifty years old.

One thing is certain: once you've owned a Citroën DS, nothing will ever match it in terms of ride quality, comfort, sheer driving pleasure and charisma. You have been warned!

APPENDIX ONE
PRODUCTION FIGURES

TOTAL PRODUCTION FIGURES

Year	Saloons	Breaks	Cabriolets	Total
1955	69			69
1956	9868			9868
1957	28593			28593
1958	52416			52416
1959	66931			66931
1960	78914	4290	1	83205
1961	72955	4480	162	77597
1962	77487	5339	212	83035
1963	86734	6501	245	93476
1964	78972	6223	184	85379
1965	82965	6222	130	89314
1966	92582	6855	136	99561
1967	94611	7211	91	101904
1968	75218	6547	95	81860
1969	75519	6652	47	82218
1970	96710	6883	40	103633
1971	78156	6159	19	84328
1972	86243	6240		92483
1973	90083	6907		96990
1974	33952	6087		40039
1975	772	75		847
TOTAL	1,359,750	92671	1365	1,455,746

SLOUGH PRODUCTION FIGURES
(INCLUDED IN TOTAL PRODUCTION)

Year	Number produced
1956	266
1957	995
1958	590
1959	990
1960	2154
1961	718
1962	459
1963	1163
1964	797
1965	338
1966	197

TOTAL: 8667
6736 of which were home sales

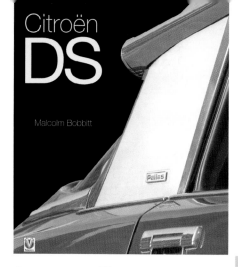

Citroën
DS

Malcolm Bobbitt

APPENDIX TWO
ORIGINAL SPECIFICATIONS

Pallas

ESSENTIAL DATA
DS19

Chassis: platform and skeleton frame; twin leading and trailing arms, anti-roll bars fore and aft; all-round hydropneumatic suspension. Rack & pinion steering, hydraulically powered. Turning circle 447in (11354mm), left, 429in (10897mm) right. Michelin X tyres, 165x400 front, 155x400 rear. Other than French-built cars equipped with 165x400 front and rear. Brakes inboard front discs, 10in outboard drums at rear, fully powered all-round.

Engine: 1911cc four cylinders inline; bore & stroke 78mmx100mm ohv, compression ratio 7.5:1. Water-cooled. Weber dual choke carburettor, maximum power 75bhp@3000rpm.

Transmission: single plate dry clutch with hydraulic actuation; four-speed gearbox.

Dimensions: wheelbase 123in (3125mm), track 59.1in (1500mm) front, 51.2in (1300mm) rear; overall length 190.5in (4838mm); overall width 70.5in (1790mm); height 57.9in (1470mm); kerb weight 2679-2932lbs (1215-1330kg).

Performance: Maximum speed 86.5mph, fuel consumption 24-29mpg.

ID19 (AS DS19 EXCEPT FOR THE FOLLOWING)
Chassis: Turning circle 426in (10820mm).

Engine: Solex single choke carburettor, maximum power 66bhp@4500rpm.

Performance: Maximum speed 82.6mph, fuel consumption 26-30mpg.
NB: Saloons built after September 1967 have an overall length of 191.9in (4874mm), overall width of 71in (1803mm), front track 59.7in (1516mm) and rear track 51.8in (1316mm)

BREAKS (AS DS19 EXCEPT FOR THE FOLLOWING)
Dimensions: Overall length 196.5in (4990mm); after 1967 197.9in (5026mm); height 60.2in (1530mm).

Engine specifications
DS
DS19, 1911cc, 11CV, 75bhp@4500rpm
DA, 1911cc, 11CV, 83bhp@4500rpm
DY,1985cc, 11CV, 90bhp@5250rpm
DY2, 1985cc, 11CV, 103bhp@5500rpm
DY3, 1985cc, 11CV, 108bhp@5500rpm

DS21, DX, 2175cc, 12CV, 109bhp@5500rpm
DX2, 2175cc, 12CV, 115bhp@5500rpm
DX3 (fuel injection), 2175cc, 12CV, 139bhp@5250rpm

DS23, DX4, 2347cc, 13CV, 124bhp@5500rpm
DX5 (fuel injection), 2347cc, 13CV, 141bhp@5500rpm

ID
ID19, 11D 1911cc, 11CV, 62bhp@4000rpm
DM, 1911cc, 11CV, 66bhp@4500rpm, later uprated to 66bhp@4500rpm
DM, 1911cc, 11CV, 75bhp@4500rpm (Sept. 1964 to Sept. 1965)
DE, 1911cc, 11CV, 81bhp@4750rpm
DS, 1911cc, 11CV, 83bhp@4500rpm
DV, 1985cc, 11CV, 84bhp@5250rpm
DV2, 1985cc, 11CV, 91bhp@5500rpm

D Spécial DV3, 1985cc, 11CV, 98bhp@5500rpm
DY2, 1985cc, 11CV, 103bhp@5500rpm

D Super & D Spécial DY3, 1985cc, 11CV, 108bhp@5500rpm

D Super5 DX2, 2175cc, 12CV, 115bhp@5500rpm

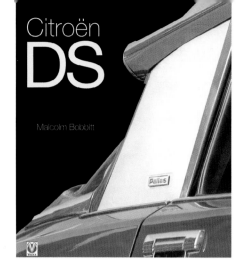

APPENDIX THREE
CLUBS, SPECIALISTS & CONTACTS

Throughout Europe there are countless enthusiast clubs, plus some in Australia, New Zealand, South Africa, the Americas, Japan, and elsewhere in the world. Because there are also numerous DS specialists, the following details are for the UK only. Readers in other countries should contact their local clubs (details available on the internet) for current information regarding specialists and events.

The club catering for UK enthusiasts is the Citroën Car Club, PO Box 348, Steyning, West Sussex, BN44 3XN, tel: 07000 248258, fax 08700 940516. The club's web site is www.citroën carclub.org.uk; this contains the latest information and contact details.

UK SPECIALISTS

Dave Ashworth for Citroën
Cowley Road, Blackpool
Lancs FY4 4NE
Tel: 01253 696294, fax: 01253 697310
email: mrcitroen@hotmail.com
Sales, service, parts, restorations

Andrew Brodie Engineering Ltd
Unit 50 Sapcote Centre
374 High Road
London NW10
Tel: 020 8459 3725, fax: 020 8451 4379
www.brodie.co.uk
Parts and servicing

Centreville Garage
Chapman Street, Shields Road
Newcastle-upon-Tyne NE6 2XT
Tel: 0191 276 3730
www.centrevillegarage.com
Sales, service, parts and restoration

The Citroën DS Wedding Car Service
Tel: 07974 7656444
www.silver-deesse.co.uk
Wedding car hire

Classique Citroën
Tel: 07941 692340
email: josgarage@compuserve.com
Importer of cars from France

Classic Citroën Parts
1 Park centre, Station Road
Horsforth
Leeds LS18 5NX
Tel/fax: 0113 258 5791
Parts: callers by appointment only

DS World Ltd
Unit 74 Chelsea Bridge Business Centre
326-340 Queenstown Road
London SW8 4NE
Tel: 020 7498 7111, fax: 020 7622 0472
Sales, parts, repairs, servicing and restorations

French Classics Ltd
Tel: 01474 703125, fax: 01474 703129
www.frenchclassics.co.uk
Sales and servicing

Heritage Restoration
London TW8 0NS
Tel: 02085 601264/07734 599400
email: heritagerestoration@btconnect. com
DS panels and chassis repair service

Longstone Classic Tyres
Tel: 0845 60 60 601
Tyres, including Michelin classic range

Medway Citroën
Tel: 01634 849609
email: medwaycitroen@btclick.com
Sales, service & parts

Paris Autos
Unit 18 Adswood Industrial Estate
Adswood Road
Stockport SK3 8LF
Tel: 0161 477 6030/3249
Parts and servicing

P. D. Gough & Co Ltd,
The Old Foundry, Common Lane
Watnall
Nottingham NG16 1HD
Tel: 0115 938 2241, fax: 0115 945 9162

www.pdgough.com
Exhaust systems

Pleiades
20 Glatton Road
Sawtry
Cambs PE28 5SY
Tel: 01487 831239, fax: 01487 832444
*Servicing and repairs or Citroën
hydraulic parts*

Southern Continental
320A Coldharbour Lane
Brixton
London SW9 8SE
Tel: 020 7274 8233/4
Service and repairs

Tinsnail
Central Works
Bridge Road
Worthing
West Sussex BN14 7BU
Tel: 01903 823880
www.tinsnail.co.uk
Sales, servicing and restorations

Vantage
Unit 3, Riverside Business Park
Lyon Road, Merton
London SW19 2RL
Tel: 020 8241 2202/8544 9998
Parts

This publication has a number of blank spaces in which appropriate companies/organisations can advertise.

Call us on 01305 260068 for details

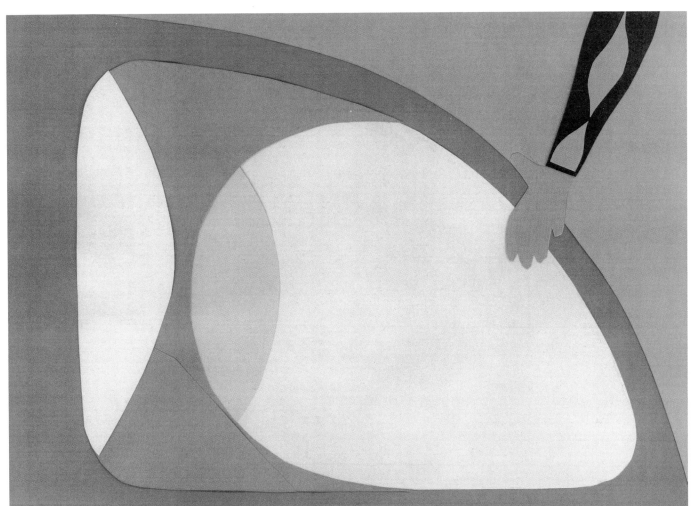

ANDREW BRODIE ENGINEERING LTD CITROEN SPECIALISTS
TEL UK +44 (0) 2084593725   WWW.BRODIE.CO.UK

Citroën **DS**

INDEX